ALBERT P. WHI[
141 RHODE ISLAND RD
LAKEVILLE, MA 02347
10/89

TELE-MISSIONS INTERNATIONAL, INC.
PARK AVENUE & KINGS HIGHWAY
VALLEY COTTAGE, NEW YORK 10989
(914) 268-3000

ECKERD

BY **Charles Paul Conn**:

BIOGRAPHY:

The New Johnny Cash
No Easy Game (with Terry Bradshaw)
Kathy (with Barbara Miller)
Julian Carroll of Kentucky
Hooked On a Good Thing (with Sammy Hall)
Just Off Chicken Street (with Floyd McClung)
Battle for Africa (with Brother Andrew)
The Power of Positive Students
    (with H. William Mitchell)
Eckerd

INSPIRATIONAL:

Making It Happen
Believe! (with Richard M. DeVos)
The Magnificent Three (with Nicky Cruz)
FatherCare

BUSINESS:

The Possible Dream
The Winner's Circle
An Uncommon Freedom
Promises to Keep

ECKERD

JACK ECKERD
and *Charles Paul Conn*

Fleming H. Revell Company
Old Tappan, New Jersey

Library of Congress Cataloging in-Publication Data

Eckerd, Jack M., 1913-
Eckerd.

1. Eckerd, Jack M., 1913-   . 2. Florida—
Biography. 3. Politicians—Florida—Biography.
4. Businessmen—Florida—Biography. 5. Christian
biography—Florida. I. Conn, Charles Paul.
II. Title.
CT275.E34A3 1987 975.9'06'0924 [B]   87-4787
ISBN 0-8007-1532-2

All rights reserved. No part of this publication may be reproduced, stored in a
retrieval system, or transmitted in any form by any means—electronic, mechanical,
photocopy, recording, or any other—except for brief quotations in printed reviews,
without the prior permission of the publisher.

Copyright © 1987 by Jack Eckerd and Charles Paul Conn
Published by the Fleming H. Revell Company
Old Tappan, New Jersey 07675
Printed in the United States of America

The Lord has blessed many of us with happy marriages, and the ending of this book affirms my good fortune. But it doesn't adequately speak to the love, understanding and respect Ruth and I have for each other. This book is dedicated to my wife, Ruth, who is largely responsible for the success of our marriage.

Acknowledgments

This book is not meant to be any sort of definitive statement of my life, and it would be foolish of me to try to acknowledge all those people who have been important to me over the years. There are simply too many of them to begin listing names.

I must say, however, that should I ever have the occasion to say "thanks" to everyone, the list will be a long one.

First, there would be the employees of the company—all those associates of Jack Eckerd Corporation who were largely responsible for my financial success.

Then there are the employees of the Eckerd Foundation, whose dedication to serving troubled youth far outweighs the monetary rewards I might be able to give them.

I would want to thank the thousands of political supporters who helped me in every campaign, never asking what was in it for them.

And I owe much to my personal staff, who put up with me in good times and bad, and who show such flexibility in shifting from one project to another.

I have had the good fortune to have several truly good friends, and they have meant much to me. They know who they are and wouldn't expect me to call their names.

I will make one exception to the no-names rule: my children. They are too much the joy of my life to omit naming them, each one, and thanking God for them. As Ruth has often said, we have a "mine, yours, ours" family of seven children. There is my son Bill and my daughter Rosemary Lassiter, both living in Pennsylvania. Ruth brought into my life her son Jim Swann and daughters Kathy Short and Terrell Clark, all of Florida. Together we claim Rick Eckerd, of New York, and Nancy Hart, who lives right here in Clearwater.

I look forward to always having an active household. Their mother's cooking always keeps them coming home again!

Preface

I never expected to write a book. If I had, I would have kept better records, maybe even made a few notes, through all these seventy-plus years.

During the years that we were building the Eckerd Corporation, we ran a lean, no-frills operation, and in those days I definitely thought of a public relations office as a frill—so I didn't even bother to save clippings from the newspapers, much less all the little personal things.

If I had known I would write a book someday, I might have been more careful about that sort of thing. It is probably just as well I didn't, because this book is not a history of my life, and it certainly is not a history of the Eckerd Corporation. It is a personal statement, a recollection of some of the things that have happened in my past.

I decided to do this book for a single reason: something has happened in my life in recent years that I believe to be worth sharing. In the last few years, I have learned what it means to "know God" in a way that I had never experienced before, and I feel compelled to talk about it.

I am aware that religious experience is a private matter, and I do not presume that I am an expert on the subject. On the other hand, my life has been public in many ways, whether or not I wished it to be, and it is only right that my religious experience should also be made part of the public record. I am doing this book because I don't think I have a right to keep my newfound personal faith a matter of private knowledge. I think I have an obligation to share it.

So this book comes from that feeling. It is an informal story of some of the things that have happened in my life, which now, looking back, seem to me to be significant.

I hope you enjoy reading it.

JACK ECKERD

Introduction

J ack Eckerd may be the youngest seventy-three-year-old man in the country.

He is a legendary figure in the business world, a senior statesman in the Florida political community, and exerts a major influence in each of the several arenas in which he operates.

Eckerd is a full-dimensioned citizen of the twentieth century. He has been around for most of it and has always squeezed all the juice he can from its diverse opportunities.

He was a barnstorming pilot in the days of open cockpits, Lucky Lindbergh, and cow-pasture airports.

He was among the eager young GIs who signed up to fight as soon as they heard about Pearl Harbor and who finished the war halfway around the world.

He jumped headlong into the booming postwar economy of the fifties, with all its risks and uncertainties, and helped pioneer an aggressive brand of marketing that put the word *entrepreneur* into the American vocabulary.

He built two broken-down stores into the nation's largest drug-store chain and literally made his name a household word.

As an untested rookie, he challenged the political establishment in Florida, almost overnight establishing a political clout that is still potent today.

In his so-called "retirement," he runs and finances a 600-employee charitable foundation, heads up a statewide political cam-paign, supervises the management of Florida's prison industries, works behind the scenes on a few boards and committees, and still finds time and energy to play tennis a couple of times a week.

Early every day Jack Eckerd goes into his office to work, and he frequently stays after the younger staff members have departed. It is a habit of many years; he says he is not a workaholic and has never been one, but others disagree. They say the Jack Eckerd we see in 1987, despite his impressive appetite for hard work and bottom-line results, is a more relaxed, mellow version of the earlier man. If that is true, he says, it is because he has finally learned the hardest lesson of his life: how to come to terms with who he is and, more important, the real purpose of living.

On April 30, 1986, an era in American retail marketing passed, when Jack Eckerd cut his formal ties to the Jack Eckerd Corporation, as he and other shareholders sold the company to a Merrill Lynch investor group and the firm's management team.

In selling his last shares of the company he had built, Jack Eckerd also resigned as a member of the board of directors, a move that was motivated by a strong desire to avoid any conflict of interest with his duty to represent the shareholders as a nonmanagement member of the board in this transaction. So the buy out ends his formal participation in the company's affairs in any way.

When the buy out occurred, the local newspapers danced out some of their most glowing adjectives to praise him. The Tampa *Tribune* wrote: "Eckerd epitomizes the storybook image of a benevolent American capitalist . . . [he] has donated his time, energy, and millions of dollars to causes that reach far beyond the checkout counters of the drugstore chain. It was not enough for Eckerd simply to make money. He put it to work raising a kingdom full of larger-than-life accomplishments."

Eckerd is a man temperamentally ill-equipped for reviewing and rehashing his own life. He refers to that as "looking back," and he does not like to do it. He once told a television interviewer, "The only way I can stay sane is to never look back." His wife, Ruth, describes him this way: "He has a marvelous way of leaving things behind him. He is not an 'if-only' person; he never looks back. Even on the tennis court, when we play mixed doubles, I'll sometimes mutter 'I wish I hadn't missed that shot,' and his attitude is 'What

difference does it make? You can't undo it, so let's just move ahead.' "

Even for a man so disinclined to look back, the severing of his last ties with a company he founded thirty-five years ago seems a fitting time to pause and take stock.

The story he is now willing to review, in this informal retrospective, is a wide-ranging one, with the energy and diversity of a man who never seems to sit still for very long. It is the story of the pilot/tycoon/candidate/philanthropist/corporate executive/public servant who is Jack Eckerd.

He is telling it now, not just because he wants us to know where he has been, but also the most important discoveries of his life—including the biggest discovery of all, a certainty about what it all means in the end.

CHARLES PAUL CONN

ECKERD

1

Few things would have been more natural than for me to spend my life in the drugstore business.

My father owned and managed drugstores; my older brothers did the same; I even had two nephews in the drugstore business. I practically grew up in drugstores, and it seems predictable, with hindsight, that I would eventually make my living in them; but that is certainly not where I was headed fifty years ago. I had something rather more exotic in mind: I wanted to be an airline pilot.

I started flying in 1932, in a cow pasture a few miles outside Erie, Pennsylvania. I loved it. It was during the early, romantic days of aviation—only five years after Lindbergh's famous transatlantic flight—and when I fell in love with flying, I fell hard.

I was a college student at the time, attending classes at an Erie extension campus of the University of Pittsburgh. The scholarly life was not suited to my restless nature, and that first year of college turned out to be my last. The classroom bored me. I was confident that there were lots of exciting things waiting out there for me, but learning algebra was not one of them.

Learning to fly was a different matter. I found an airstrip in the little town of Fairview, just outside Erie, where a pilot named Neil McCray gave lessons. McCray was only about thirty years old. He owned a couple of planes and offered a ten-hour beginner's course, which covered everything right up to and including a pilot's license. I signed up for the course and did my ten hours in a biplane called a Great Lakes trainer. It had an open cockpit with two seats, fore and aft; the instructor sat behind the student, and both wore goggles against the onrushing wind. There were wings above and below us, with guy wires holding them together, and a single propeller on the nose. We had everything but the silk scarf.

After ten hours in that trainer, I was hooked. I was determined to find a way to fly on a regular basis and in a flash of inspiration conceived a plan to do so: I would offer to be my father's private pilot.

My father owned and managed several drugstores. He had been in the drugstore business since 1898, fifteen years before I was born, and had built a small chain of about a dozen stores. He literally had two families; he had four children by his first wife, who had died as a young woman. After twenty years as a widower, he had married again, and his new bride had given him three more children, one of whom was me.

When I was ten years old, living in Philadelphia, my mother died. My father could not meet the demands of his business and still be a full-time parent, so I was sent, at the age of twelve, to a prep school in New Jersey. Dad came up to see me a couple of times, decided the prep-school life was not tough enough for me, and transferred me the next year to Culver Military Academy. Culver was tough enough.

During my Culver days my father moved to Erie. I first went "home" to Erie on my Christmas vacation in 1926, getting off the train from Culver in a blinding snowstorm, without the slightest idea where to go. I didn't know where we lived and had lost my father's letter telling me how to get there. I finally found the house, with the help of a friend, but I'd had a cold and not very reassuring introduction to the town I was to call home.

There was never any pressure on me to enter the family business. My father let me know I was welcome to work for him, but warned me to expect no special privileges as the boss's son. "I don't care if you go into this business with me or not," he said. "But if you do, you're going to work harder than anyone else around here, I'll tell you that! If your name is Eckerd, that means you come earlier and stay later. You've got a job if you want it, but I'm not going to have you messing up my business just because you're my son."

The funny thing was, I really *did* want to work for him. Our relationship was never a particularly close one; he was already in his early forties when I was born and was gone so much of the time that we never developed the intimacy some fathers and sons share. But when he was home, he was a good father. He loved baseball and enjoyed taking me to games with him. He always was firm and fair with me, refused to spoil me by giving me too much, and allowed me plenty of options in life. I loved and admired him—and I wanted to work for him, which I did, returning to Erie after high school to attend college and work in his drugstore business.

The problem with working for my father was the same as the problem with attending classes: boredom. One was about as dull as the other, especially after I met Neil McCray and got my first taste of flying. It is difficult for a pharmacy stockroom to compete with the glamour of an open cockpit, especially for an eighteen-year-old.

That was when I decided my father needed a pilot.

My proposal to him was this: he would put up the money, and I would buy an airplane; I would stay on his payroll and would fly him wherever he wanted to go. He was a busy man, I argued, always traveling to his drugstores, some of which were several hundred miles away. Why not travel faster and arrive fresher, by making use of modern technology and a mechanically talented son?

To my considerable surprise, he thought it over and agreed—a tribute more to his open-mindedness than to my powers of persuasion. It was up to me to choose a plane. I would have preferred a plane with an open cockpit, like the Great Lakes trainer, but I knew my father would never go for it. This man was in his early sixties; we would fly from Erie to destinations as far away as Wilmington, Delaware; Elmira, New York; and Charlotte, North Carolina. Private aviation itself was in a very early and primitive state, and the pilot to whom he entrusted his life had barely learned to fly. I was smart enough to realize that, on top of all the rest, he was not going to fly wearing goggles in the open air, like some aging Red Baron, so I gave up on the idea of an open cockpit.

Instead I found a single-engine Stinson, a little four-seater with a closed cabin. It was a high-wing monoplane, with a 245 horsepower engine, and would fly at about 105 miles per hour, with no wind. He paid $7,000 for it.

For the next two years, I happily flew my father back and forth from Erie to all the cities where he had stores. It was a good arrangement for both of us. Looking back, it seems remarkable that my father would have such confidence in me and my little Stinson, especially considering the distances we flew, often crossing the Allegheny Mountains, with navigational equipment and ground support services far more primitive than we have today. But he never flinched. He would sit back there and read and think nothing of it, while I picked my way across the landscape, often hoping I knew what I was doing, always loving every minute of it.

The only downside of the arrangement came when my father stayed at home. When he was not traveling, I worked in the drugstores in Erie, usually down in the basement, filling orders. The more I flew, the harder it was to be happy in the basement of a drugstore, and my restlessness intensified.

I also had a growing awareness of how little I knew about flying. The more hours I logged in that Stinson, the more I realized I needed better training. It is said that the most dangerous time for a new pilot is after getting a license and before logging 200 hours— that is, the period before he learns just how much he does *not* know. I had a couple of forced landings in fields, survived a few close calls in that Stinson, and began to understand how inexperienced I was. I wanted to go to a good flight school and learn how to do it right.

In those days, the commercial airline industry was just developing; United Airlines was using Stinson trimotors for passenger service. Not having the steady supply of pilots from military and private aviation, which they have today, the airlines trained their own.

United Airlines, Boeing, and Pratt-Whitney, all part of the same company at that time, operated a school in Alameda, California, for commercial pilots, which were then called "transport pilots." In 1934, there was no better training available anywhere in the country.

I was so wrapped up in flying that I could not imagine myself in any other occupation. I explained to my father: "Dad, this drugstore business just doesn't do anything for me, and I love to fly." I told him how badly I needed more training—he didn't disagree—and told him about the school for transport pilots in California.

"Will you send me out there for a year?"

"Sure," he said.

"Can I take the Stinson with me?"

"Might as well," he said, "it's no good to me around here. You're the only one who knows how to fly the thing."

So I took off to California, me and my Stinson, bouncing across the country at 300 miles per hop, with barely enough money to get me there, but a surplus of self-confidence. The trip was scheduled to take four and a half days from Erie to Alameda.

Just outside Saint Louis, I got caught in a blinding rainstorm that neither I nor my plane could handle. While making a forced landing in a farmer's field, I turned the plane over and half-crashed it, nose down, in the mud. I climbed out, shaken but unhurt; the plane itself was intact, but the propeller was badly bent. I took it off and hitched a ride back into Saint Louis, to Lambert Field, to get the prop straightened out.

I wrote it down to luck that it happened where it did. Lambert Field was one of the earliest centers for aviation in the country; it was the home base for Charles Lindbergh and a hotbed of seat-of-the-pants, barnstorming young flyers. It was one of the few places in the country where a rookie pilot could walk in, covered with mud, with a bent prop in his arms, and get the kind of help he needed.

The crew at Lambert told me they could fix my prop, but it would cost $100, which was substantially more than I had. It was impossible to call home and ask for the money without explaining what had happened, and I knew that my father's confidence in me, impressive as it was, had its limits. *If he learns I have crashed this Stinson out here in Missouri,* I figured, *he will tell me to come home before I kill myself.*

So I called Bill, my half-brother. It was not the first or the last time I took advantage of having brothers who were themselves old enough to be my father, and they always came through for me. "Hey, Bill," I shouted through the long-distance lines. "How about wiring me a hundred bucks? I bent a prop out here in Saint Louis, and I don't wanna bother Dad." Bill sent the money. I got the prop straightened, put it back on the plane, and was on my way again.

When I got to Alameda, I found the airfield, right on the edge of Oakland Bay, landed, and taxied up to the little office right on the strip. I walked in and said, "My name is Eckerd. I'm from Pennsylvania; you should have a letter from me somewhere. I'm here to join the class starting next week."

The man behind the desk looked through some files and found my letter. "Okay, Eckerd, glad to have you. How'd you come out?"

"I flew."

"You flew?! From Pennsylvania?" It was more a statement of surprise than a question.

"Yeah."

"What did you fly in?"

I pointed out the window at my little plane. "That Stinson sitting out there."

He pushed his chair back, scratched his head, and finally looked back at me. "If you flew that thing all the way out here from Pennsylvania, what are you going to school for?"

"Because I've almost killed myself three or four times, and I wanna learn to really fly. I want to fly the airlines."

The course lasted a year. There were fourteen students in the class, all of us young and somewhat on the crazy edge. We all stayed in a boarding house together and flew all day and caroused most of the night. Speed was our recreational drug; we couldn't get enough of it. I bought an old motorcycle for seventy-five bucks and almost killed myself ramming it through a plate-glass window. Many times I think the Lord must have been with me, or I wouldn't have survived that year—it surely wasn't my intelligence that got me through; I was twenty years old and full of myself. By all accounts I shouldn't have lived to see twenty-one.

After our class completed the course, I passed the exam and received my transport pilot's license. I thought that license was an automatic guarantee of a job flying with United Airlines. I presented myself to the personnel officer the next day: "Okay, I'm ready to go to work." The officer noted my name and credentials, approved my freshly minted license, then told me I would have to wait until there was an opening for a pilot. It might be as long as a year before they had a slot available, he explained. I would just have to hang around Alameda with the rest of the guys and wait my turn.

I did not want to wait. I had been in California over a year and was restless again, so I decided to head back east and see what turned up there. I had recently heard from my father and knew he had been in Los Angeles for a couple of months. I called him and told him I was ready to go back home to Pennsylvania. He was ready to head back, too, he said; so why not fly the Stinson down to L. A. and pick him up, and we could go back together?

We flew out of California early one morning, crossing southern Arizona, when I looked ahead and saw a cloud bank with a slightly miscast color. *What are these clouds doing out here in the middle of the desert?* I wondered, when suddenly we were in a dust storm, almost completely blinded. I dropped lower and lower, trying to get under the storm enough to see the east-west highway I was following. No good. It got so bad I finally had to land in a field near a little town. We found a way into town, stayed all night, came back to our plane the next day, and flew on.

That was not an uncommon experience for private pilots in the 1930s. Most of the time we flew rivers and railroads and highways, strictly visual navigation, depending on towns and other landmarks to guide the way. The Stinson had an old turn-and-bank navigational system, with a radio that often did not work. It was possible to navigate by following radio beams, but little planes like ours couldn't pick them up very well; they were not at all useful except within twenty miles of an airport. Otherwise, we trusted our eyes. It was easy to get lost, especially over the vast empty space of the West. We often lost track of where we were, and spotting a town below, would reorient ourselves by buzzing down low enough to read the signs on the railroad station.

The highest and most efficient altitude in the Stinson was 12,000 feet, but the need for visual navigation or the presence of high-altitude weather systems often kept us much lower than that. Our top speed was just over 100 miles per hour, and when we were fighting a strong headwind, we barely got there faster than the automobiles below us.

Even with all that, it was wonderful. After that first lesson with Neil McCray, in the Fairview cow pasture, I was hooked on flying, and I still am today. But at least I had decided, by 1935, that aviation was not where my future lay. I returned to Erie, my wanderlust partially and temporarily satisfied, and went back to work in the family business.

When I returned, it was with a new attitude toward the drugstore business and my future in it. I no longer saw it as a trap to avoid and gradually developed professional curiosity about what made it work and how it could be improved. With my system purged of the urge to be an airline pilot, I began to warm to the idea of a career in drugstores.

When I returned to Erie, at first I worked for my two older half-brothers, who owned a few stores in Pennsylvania and Indiana, and for my father, who had about fifteen in New York, Delaware, and North Carolina. As I moved up, literally and figuratively, from the basement to the main floor, he relied on me more and more for management duties, and I evidently responded well to the challenge and his confidence in me.

In many ways, my father was a hard-nosed, no-nonsense task-

master. He always insisted that I work hard, and he pushed me
pretty fast, after I indicated a serious interest in the business. He was
tough on me, but he also gave me plenty of room to make my own
mistakes and learn my own lessons. He didn't believe a father ought
always to protect his children from their own stupidity, and I respected him for that.

For example: early in the period when I was serving as his pilot,
all his employees went to the shores of Lake Erie for a company
picnic on a beautiful summer evening. I was scheduled to fly him
from Erie to Detroit, a three-hour trip, early the next morning. At
the picnic, we had the usual hot dogs and kegs of beer, and I was a
typically intemperate young man who enjoyed my beer. I drank my
share, then a bit more, and finally entirely too much. My father just
sat there, watched, and didn't say a word as I drank myself silly.

Early the next morning he pounded on my door. Predictably, I
had a monstrous hangover; I was sick; I hoped he would mercifully
cancel the trip or at least postpone it until I could recover a bit. No
such luck. When I finally opened my bedroom door, he was brisk,
matter-of-fact, all business: "On your feet, Jack, I'm going to Detroit, and you're going to fly me." I responded the only way I could:
"Yessir."

That was the longest, most nauseous trip I ever flew. My father
was making me suffer, knew exactly what he was doing, and did it
for a reason. He never mentioned my drinking at all. I got the
message, loud and clear, and he didn't need to say a word.

But laced through his toughness was a bedrock confidence in me,
and it communicated. Even in that incident, while he refused to let
me off the hook, he did not hesitate to climb into the plane and fly
with me to Detroit. He knew I was young and foolish, but he also
knew I could get the job done. He trusted me, and I sensed it, and
that was important.

It's a good thing he didn't know what we know today about the
influence of alcohol on a pilot's coordination, though.

During the six years after I returned from California, I gradually
learned the business. My father had a general manager in Erie who

helped supervise the entire operation, and I learned a lot from both of them. When the manager died, in the late 1930s, I began to assume day-to-day responsibility for operation of the stores.

I also met and married a girl in Wilmington, and we soon bought a house and started a family. I was working hard and saving my money, and in 1940 bought 25 percent of the ownership of two local stores from my father. I was obviously settling down.

Then the war came.

2

Like most people in my generation, I have no difficulty recalling the moment I heard that Pearl Harbor had been bombed. Like everyone else, I also knew what the news meant: the war was now *our* war, and life was going to change for all of us.

I was twenty-nine years old, with a wife and daughter, living in Wilmington. My wife and I were sitting in the living room on that Sunday morning in December of 1941; the radio was on, and we heard what must have been the first news broadcast of the Pearl Harbor disaster.

My first reaction was pure anger, not just at the Japanese for attacking us, but also at whoever allowed such a thing to happen. How could we be so dumb as to let them do such a thing to us? As far as I was concerned, Japan was a second-rate developing country, and their getting a jump on us infuriated me. Someone must have been asleep at the switch, I figured, and it made me mad.

My second reaction was a more personal one: there was a war on, and I wanted to be in it.

I was still a licensed transport pilot, though I had not flown much in recent years, and I realized that my best shot at doing something significant was in the Army Air Corps. After Pearl Harbor, I began to hear appeals for anyone with 1,000 hours of flying experience to register for a government refresher course; my logbook showed over 3,000 hours, so I signed up. The refresher course, which was taught at DuPont Airfield, right in Wilmington, lasted three months. By the time I had completed it, I had regained the sharp appetite for flying that I had felt when I was a teenager.

The AAF wanted me to sign on as a flight instructor. I learned I was to work at a base in Texas, training younger men to be pilots, who would then fly off to have the real fun fighting the war. I thought, holy smokes, wouldn't that be monotonous—sitting down there in Texas at a training base, flying traffic patterns around an airport until the war was over!

At that time, Neil McCray, who had taught me to fly ten years earlier, was based in Wilmington as part of the Air Transport Command. The ATC was an outfit whose primary duty was to ferry planes around the country and to Europe, India, and Africa, moving them from the factories to the combat zones. Neil came to visit me one night, and obviously he was enjoying his work, flying B-26s all over the country.

"Neil," I said, "I've been thinking about this thing of being a flight instructor, and I don't like the sound of it. Any chance I could get into the ATC?"

"Sure," he said. "Just go down to the base and tell the personnel office that's what you want to do. They can't send you to Texas to teach rookiesif you already have orders with the ATC."

So I did. I walked into the personnel office the next day, with my logbook in hand, tossed it on the officer's desk, and told him I was available for duty. The logbook showed a pretty impressive record of flying time, and I thought he would be glad to sign me up. But the man barely looked at the log. "Sorry," he told me, "we're not hiring any pilots right now." End of conversation.

I tried to argue, but he was a brick wall. I stomped out of that office, furious, thinking, *This guy's gotta be nuts. There's a war on, and I have 3,000 hours of flight time, and this guy says they don't need pilots!*

In one of those moments of incredibly good timing, Neil McCray happened to walk by as I was standing outside the personnel office, trying to decide what to do next. I told him what had happened.

"Why don't you go see the commanding officer?" he suggested. "You got nothing to lose—might as well give it a try."

So I went immediately to the office of the base commander, a Colonel Black. I was ushered in to see him after about a ten-minute wait. I gave him my file, but he glanced at the Culver Academy ring I was wearing.

He interrupted me: "When were you in Culver, Eckerd?"

"I got out in thirty, sir."

"Well, good for you. I'm a Culver man myself. Got out in twenty-two."

With that he reached across his desk, picked up a telephone, shouted to what must have been a startled personnel officer, "I've got Eckerd down here. I'm sending him over. Hire him," and hung up.

It was one of those little things that change your life. I marched straight back into the personnel office, filled out a few forms, and left as an operational pilot in the Air Transport Command, where I stayed until the war was over.

I was based at Newcastle Army Air Base, in Wilmington. We flew all kinds of planes; it was a pilot's dream. We would deliver a plane to an air base, then return the fastest way, sometimes by train or airline, but often by flying "deadhead" back to Wilmington in military aircraft. Mostly we flew the B-26 bomber, which was supposedly one of the most dangerous planes in the war. It had such stubby little wings that it was called the Flying Prostitute—no visible means of support. We flew that plane so much that we actually grew fond of it, sawed-off wings and all.

The ATC was not a combat assignment, but it was not without its excitement or its hazards. As the war progressed, we made fewer flights to United States bases, instead spending most of our time delivering planes to England, for use in the European theater. The standard run was from Wilmington to Prestwick, Scotland, in a B-26. We flew four-man crews: pilot, copilot, navigator, and engineer.

The flight to Prestwick took only about twenty hours' air time, but in those days it was a four-day trip. We made three stops: Goose Bay (Labrador); a landing strip called BW1, at the foot of Greenland; and Reykjavik, Iceland. We would overnight and refuel in those places, fly into Prestwick on the fourth day, and usually be turned around and headed back to the States within twenty-four hours. The standard ride home was in the back of an empty transport plane, eighty or ninety guys sitting or lying on the floor. I hated those trips back; the only other way home was to fly a ''war-weary'' plane, which had been shot up pretty badly, and I did that whenever I could, just to avoid the cattle-car ride in the back of those C-54 transports.

The worst part of the run to Prestwick was flying into BW1. It was a desolate place, always covered with ice; to get in, we flew into one of those fjords and landed on a metal mat. The approach was over water all the way in, landing right into a mountain of ice. We flew in, landed, the ground crews turned the plane around, and the next morning we flew out again the same way we came in.

We had to use every inch of runway at BW1; the strip was short and was built with about a 3 percent incline. With that slight pitch, the plane landed uphill, which helped slow us down, and we took off going downhill with a full load of fuel, which gave it a bit more speed. Coming in was the treacherous part, because we couldn't overshoot the runway; down in that fjord, there was no such thing as going around again. We had to get it right the first time.

The first trip or two a new pilot flew into BW1 was pretty scary. My first approach was a disaster; I actually didn't land at all. We rarely had a complete set of radio equipment in those planes, because they were going to be used in England, and the British navigational equipment was installed over there. On my first trip across as a pilot, I was assigned to fly in formation with another plane, which had a colonel on board. Because the colonel planned to bring the same plane back again, it was loaded with full radio. I was instructed to tag along with his plane, since he had all the radio equipment needed to get us into BW1.

We took off from Goose Bay right behind the colonel, but his plane was lighter and faster than ours, and when we broke through the overcast, the colonel had disappeared. We had to try to get into BW1 on our own. Somewhere just short of Greenland, I went down through the overcast to try to find the entrance to the fjord. The problem was that there were *several* fjords, all of which looked the same to me. If we headed into the wrong one, there would be no place to land and no room to turn around and fly back out. Obviously, it's important to pick the right fjord.

There was supposed to be a radio signal to identify the entrance to the BW1 fjord, but we couldn't pick it up. We finally had to turn around, embarrassed, and return to Goose Bay on our dwindling fuel supply. The next day we made it alone. We never saw that colonel again!

That particular incident was largely a result of my own inexperience, but my crew and I came even closer to disaster on another occasion when we were not at fault. We were delivering a B-24 bomber from its factory in Detroit to Karachi, India, where it was to be used in the China-Burma-India operations.

We were part of a whole air convoy of four-engine bombers, and we could see almost immediately that they were burning fuel more rapidly than they should. The route from Detroit led us down to the coast of Brazil, where we made a stop for fuel and had a final briefing before starting across the South Atlantic. On the ocean crossing, we had no stop scheduled in the Ascension Islands, as we sometimes did, but were to fly all the way to Africa in one hop.

There were about forty of us at the briefing that night in Brazil. I told the officer giving the briefing that our plane was burning excessive fuel on the run down from Detroit, but he ignored me. I asked him about the winds over the Atlantic; he said they were mild and should create no problem. "Based on the data," I persisted, "we'll be lucky if we have enough fuel to get to Africa." He made a flippant remark and dismissed my comment. We went out to the flight line and hoped for the best.

We departed at about 10:00 P.M. As we took off and left the South American coast, my engines began overheating again, as they had before. To cool them, we had to open the cowl flaps on the engines, which created more drag and caused the plane to burn more fuel.

The auxiliary fuel tanks on the B-24 were in the back, with glass gauges on the bulkhead, so the engineer could visually inspect the fuel level as it fell, like looking at water in a rain gauge. We checked those levels constantly, throughout what became a very long night. A few hours off the African coast, the engineer came up to give me the bad news: his calculations showed we were about twenty minutes short of fuel.

We called the African base to tell them we might not make it. They responded that they had us on radar and wished us luck; that's about all they could do. For the rest of the flight, we squeezed everything we could from the fuel that remained. Our altitude was about 15,000 feet, and from that I dropped the plane about fifty feet a minute, trying to nurse it in. Finally we saw the lights of the airfield and landed with no fuel showing in the gauges. As we did, one of our engines sputtered and quit, completely dry, before we could even taxi to the base at the end of the runway.

A couple of planes in our convoy went into the sea that night; we were very fortunate not to be with them.

Even with the occasional emergency, it was an enjoyable time in my life; I was flying all kinds of planes in all kinds of circumstances, and I continued that kind of duty until the end of 1943, when ''success'' almost spoiled the fun for me.

Because I had lots of flying time, and probably also because I was a few years older than most of the other guys, I was given a promotion to the position of ''air inspector.'' My new duty was to keep track of the maintenance on all our planes, see that the crews were properly trained, and that sort of thing. It was basically a desk job, easy duty, and I suppose the brass thought they were doing me a favor by giving me the assignment. But there wasn't much to it, and I hated it. All I did was keep charts. AF officers would fly in periodically and look at my charts, and if the charts were okay, they didn't check further. Every plane on the base could have been falling apart, but if the charts looked good, they were happy.

I told Colonel Black, our commanding officer, I wanted to get out of that job and get back to flying. "Okay," he said, "but if you do, you're likely to end up 'flying the Hump,' and you certainly don't want to do that."

The Hump was considered the most hazardous area in the war for noncombat pilots. It was a stretch of the Himalaya Mountains between India and China. In order to support American plane and Chinese troops in their war against the Japanese, American and British fliers shuttled supplies to them by making dangerous night flights across the most rugged mountains in the world. Flying the Hump was famous for its high casualty rates.

"You don't want to fly the Hump, do you?"

"I don't know about the Hump," I answered, "but I know I want out of this desk job."

So, sure enough, I wound up flying the Hump. I applied for additional training, was assigned to a one-month course in instrument and night flying in Saint Joseph, Missouri, and immediately afterward received orders that eventually took me to the Hump.

I was assigned to go to Nashville, Tennessee, pick up a C-46 loaded with about sixty GIs, and fly to Karachi, India. A C-46 was a fairly modern plane, one notch up from the familiar DC-3. I was given a set of sealed orders, not to be opened until I was en route to Karachi. When I opened the orders, they told me only that I was to deliver the plane and the troops to Karachi, where I would be given my next assignment.

In Karachi, I reported to headquarters, having landed at about 5:00 P.M., after all the officers had left for dinner. A sergeant was there, and I told him I wanted to get my new orders cut immediately, so I could get out of there early the next day. "Go get something to eat," he told me, "and I'll pull your paperwork and give you new orders when you get back."

I returned an hour later to find a puzzled sergeant, still studying my file. "I don't understand it, sir," he said, "but there's some kind of mistake here on your orders." I looked at the papers and to my horror discovered that I had been classified, once again, for primary duty as an air inspector! Fortunately, there had been a misprint in the classification number, and the sergeant, unfamiliar with the paperwork, didn't know what to make of it.

"Well, look, sergeant," I said, "I can't figure all this out, either. Somebody back in the States obviously made a mistake. But it says here"—and I pointed to another set of numbers—"that I'm checked out as a four-engine pilot, so why don't you just cut me a set of orders as a four-engine pilot, and I'll deliver this plane I've got to whatever base you send me to."

He shrugged, typed up a set of orders, and handed them over. The next morning I was on my way to the base at Dacca, 300 miles from the foothills of the Himalayas, with orders to fly the Hump.

When I arrived at the base, the first guy I ran into was a colonel, who spotted me and yelled from a distance, "Hey, Eckerd!" He was a friend from Wilmington, whom I had not seen since the war began, and who was now in charge of this base. He was obviously surprised to see me, as I was him.

After a few moments of small talk, he asked, "Say, Jack, weren't you an air inspector?"

"Yes, I was, colonel."

"Great!" he beamed. "We need a good air inspector!"

"Colonel," I said, "I appreciate the opportunity, but I came all the way over here because I didn't want to be an air inspector! Please don't do that to me! I'm a pilot, and all I want to do is fly."

He paused a moment. "Okay, sure. Just thought you might like a desk job."

Why is it, I wondered, *when so many people are trying to get* out *of the war, I am having such a difficult time getting* into *the war?*

From that time on, until the armistice with Japan, in late 1945, I was stationed in Dacca and flew supplies over the Hump. In a peculiar way, it was one of the best times of my life. The living conditions at that base were pretty crude, but the companionship was great, and I had never been around a group of men I liked better. It was the closest thing to pure communal living I have ever experienced. We lived in large huts with thatched roofs and bamboo slat sides, called "bashas." Each basha housed six to eight men. The floors were half dirt and half brick.

Those thatch huts were cooler and more efficient than Quonset huts would have been. Once we got accustomed to the rats running around the rafters at night, we were quite comfortable. We slept under mosquito nets, because of the constant threat of malaria.

Each crew made about three trips across the Hump each week, and every run could be very dangerous. But between trips, we had nothing to do but sit around the basha and talk, play cards, and think of different ways to eat the tough Australian beef we were fed. The casualty rates were so high—we sometimes lost two crews a week—that a certain fatalism developed among us. We didn't think about the danger much; we felt that if our time came, it came, and that atmosphere contributed to the strong kinship and camaraderie among us.

When I recall that period of my life, I marvel that I thought so rarely about God. Like virtually everyone else in that group of GI's, I was almost totally uninterested in anything religious. It might seem that men living in a situation so filled with danger and death would take time to consider the spiritual meaning of it all, but we didn't. We were typical, I think, of most young men—we were too busy living day by day to focus on questions of eternal meaning. That would eventually change for me, but it would be many years later.

We were like a big family. When anyone got a package from home, everyone shared the contents. If it was food, we all ate it until it was gone. If someone broke a shoelace, he just looked around until he found one—it didn't matter whose locker he found it in. Except for our natural desire to be home, it was a great experience. If I had not been married and felt a responsibility to my wife and child, I would have enjoyed it completely.

But we were not there to sit around the basha and swap tales; we were there to fly supplies over the Himalayas, and we did plenty of that. There were three routes across, each posing different challenges, depending on the weather and the loads we were carrying. The mountains we crossed ranged up to 20,000 feet. We flew mostly in B-24s that had been converted to carry gasoline. They had nonpressurized cabins, which means we had to wear oxygen masks all the time.

The duration of the flights varied with the weather, but during the lengthy monsoon season, it took us about eight or nine hours to get over and back. The ground crews in China would turn us around quickly; we went into the mess hall, ate a meal (usually of eggs), and flew straight out again.

Our orders were to leave behind with the Chinese as much of our unspent fuel as possible. Sometimes the weather was so bad that very little was left at all; sometimes we barely had enough in our own tanks to make it home. It was not unusual for the weather to be so bad, when we arrived over our destination at Kunming that we would have to be diverted up to Luliang or someplace else and have to find a hole in the storm to set down. On one such day, I landed and a fellow came up to the plane and asked "How much gas can you leave with us?" "Leave?" I responded. "I'm going to need a hundred and fifty more gallons from you just to get back to my base!"

The weather was so turbulent in the Himalayas that sextants and wind-drift equipment were rarely useful, so we pared down to three-man crews, with no navigators. That lightened us and let us carry more supplies. Our usual cargo was bombs and gasoline. They converted the planes by mounting 500-gallon gasoline tanks inside, where the bomb racks had been. Those B-24s were built to carry 48,000 pounds, but we often went out at 60,000 pounds. If we happened to lose an engine on takeoff, we could kiss it all good-bye. With those fuel tanks behind us, we were at least assured of a spectacular fireworks display when we hit.

The greatest hazards were presented by the fierce storms during the rainy season. Our casualty rates went up during the monsoons. We often flew in marginal conditions, far beyond the acceptable limits for normal civilian air traffic. There was a war on, so we flew. There were also losses of aircraft due to mechanical failure, since we were pushing our equipment hard, with not enough time for repairs and maintenance. Many times, the losses were caused by simple human error, either by pilots or ground crews. If a plane carrying a cargo of heavy bombs or fifty-five-gallon drums was loaded incorrectly, the plane could actually stall out on takeoff or when we hit turbulent air. It was not uncommon for a load of fifty-five-gallon drums to break loose during a storm and start bouncing around back there. That was enough to test the skill of the best pilots.

The pilots themselves were usually young and often had minimal training, and the terrain over which we flew was particularly unforgiving. We usually landed on long, narrow, crushed-rock runways, in closed-end valleys between two mountains. When a pilot made the wrong turn, while flying blind in one of those valleys, he hit the mountain; there were few second chances.

I recall one particularly bad night, coming back. We had no radar to avoid the storms. As we approached the mountain and climbed, there was so much lightning that the sky was lit up the entire time. We couldn't find a hole in the storm and had to bore right through it, bouncing around like a chip. I considered turning back, but we were past the point where that was possible. Lots of planes went down that night, but we made it through. When we landed, we found the leading edges of our wings literally had been chewed up by hailstones. I still don't know how our plane stayed in the air.

None of us who were there will ever forget when the war in the Pacific ended. I was flying a fairly routine run over to Kunming and had my headset on, when I heard the news on the radio. I landed and walked into the operations hut; they asked if I had heard the news. "You bet I did," I grinned.

"How would you like to go to Shanghai?"

Shanghai was held by the Japanese; to go there was almost like going into Berlin the day the Germans surrendered. The officer explained to me that the Allies were trying to get the Chinese Second Army into Shanghai, to accept the Japanese surrender before the Chinese Communists could get there. It sounded like fun to me and my crew. The next morning, we set out for Shanghai in our C-54, the cargo area crammed with a Chinese general and ninety soldiers, most of whom got sick in a patch of rough weather on the way over.

We landed, rolled up on the tarmac, and saw a long rank of Japanese officers standing at attention, sabers drawn, just as if they were at a parade. When I opened the door and climbed down, one of them asked courteously if he could address the Chinese general, so I went back into the plane to get him. For a long time, he didn't move from where he was sitting. "Let them wait," he finally said. "I've been waiting for many years for this, so let them wait a few minutes themselves."

I have one other vivid memory of that August day in 1945. One of the Japanese officers, saber gleaming, stepped up to me and, to my utter surprise, spoke in perfect English: "Say, captain, what do you think my chances are of getting back to the States?"

"Where are you from?" I asked incredulously.

"L.A.," he answered.

"What in the world are you doing here?"

He explained that his father had written him a letter, about a year before the war began, asking him to come back to Japan to help with the family business. He had done so and had somehow ended up here, in Shanghai, in an officer's uniform, with a finely polished saber. He repeated the question: "So—what are my chances, captain?"

"I hope about like a snowball in hell."

I was still mad at the whole Japanese army. But I have thought often about that man since then, and the crazy thing is this: chances are pretty good he *did* make it back to the States. He probably owns half of Los Angeles by now!

3

That Japanese officer and I shared at least one thing in common: we both were ready to get back to the United States.

When I returned to Wilmington, I was thirty-two years old and ready to get moving with a business career. From the moment I removed my major's uniform and became Citizen Eckerd again, I never questioned pursuing my future in the drugstore business. Like millions of other GIs, my life had been interrupted by the war, and now that it was over, I suddenly felt an urgent need to make up for lost time, to turn the page and start the next chapter.

I immediately resumed work with my father and brothers, Bill and Ken. I still owned twenty-five percent of the Wilmington stores, and my father offered to sell me the other seventy-five percent. I bought them, and leaving them under the day-to-day supervision of a top-flight manager named Andy Kirkpatrick, I went to Erie to help my brothers and my father run their stores.

My father operated his stores in the tradition of old-fashioned pharmacies. Drugstores in those days were small; retailing was more personal than it is today. Merchandise was stacked high on wall shelves or virtually hidden behind counters, and the customer had little access to it. There was no "shopping" in the sense that we have it in modern stores. The customer came in and asked a clerk for the product, and the clerk got it for him, often by pulling it down from those high shelves with a long-handled hook. A personal relationship existed between the druggist and his customer and also between the druggist and the local physicians.

My father's stores followed the traditional pattern, with one important exception: price. He was one of the original "cut-rate" (discount) druggists in the country. This practice did not endear him to his competitors: he was something of a maverick and built his business by offering discount prices to his customers. When he moved to Erie in 1898 to open his first store, he realized he needed some kind of edge to compete with the established stores which had been there for years.

Dad started with almost no investment capital. He had a cousin in the wholesale drug business, whom he persuaded to give him $600 worth of merchandise on credit, with a year to repay. He rented a storefront in Erie, set out the $600 worth of products, and saw that the shelves still looked woefully bare. Not to worry—he went back to his cousin, borrowed stacks of empty boxes and "dummy" advertising displays, and put those on the shelves to create the appearance of a fully stocked store. With that kind of operation, survival depended on his turning over his meager inventory quickly, and he did that by cutting prices.

Price cutting was practically unknown in the drugstore business, and his competitors tried to prevent wholesale suppliers from doing business with Dad. When "drummers" (salesmen) from the drug companies came to the established stores, they were warned by Dad's competitors not to deal with him. But my father's business was too brisk to ignore, so salesmen would simply avoid his store during the daytime, then come in the back door after dark, to do business with him.

The established relationships between druggists and their customers were tough to crack, making it a difficult business for a newcomer to build, but my father did it, using low prices and a time-honored Eckerd stubbornness.

At the end of World War II, however, the patterns of American retailing shifted rapidly, the drugstore business included. Vast, seismic upheavals in the American marketplace affected every type of retailing, and the profitability of small, storefront pharmacies eroded. My father had been ahead of one trend—discount prices—but there were many major sociocultural changes occurring after the war, and the future would belong to those who could anticipate and take advantage of them.

When I returned from the war, I began to participate more aggressively in the family business, and inevitably my own ideas about building a business clashed with my father's. The contrast between his old-school philosophy and my new-wave concepts crystallized in a disagreement regarding two of his stores in Jamestown, New York.

He owned two stores in Jamestown. Both were small and in cheap-rent locations. I went to Jamestown to manage the operation for Dad, but found the two smaller ones were going downhill. Just as I was wondering how to turn those stores around, a large Kresge's store in the area closed, and its building became available. It was an excellent retail location, and I decided to merge our two small drugstores into a single store at that location.

The problem was that the lease at the new site cost $1,000 a month; we were paying only $200 a month in the off locations; and my father was a strong believer in cheap rent. I told him what I proposed to do and he said, "No." Just flat no. "Son, you can't make any money paying that much rent," he said, and as far as he was concerned, that was that.

I argued the point. I argued fiercely. I explained that the stores were losing money anyway, that they were too small, that we would save on payroll costs by merging them, that we could pay the higher rent and still come out ahead because the store was so much larger and the location so much better. He still would not budge. I was getting exasperated.

"The problem is," I told my father, "that you give me all the responsibility and none of the authority! You expect me to make a profit with these stores, but you won't trust me to make the decisions!"

The answer was still no.

Now I was getting mad. It was obvious my logic was being totally ignored. So finally, I went to my trump card: "If you can't give me the authority to make this kind of decision," I declared, "I'm going to quit!"

"I wouldn't blame you if you did," he responded.

So I quit. No hard feelings. Dad just wasn't ready to give up the driver's seat.

I didn't just threaten; I really did quit. I took my savings, bought a camper-trailer, and had enough left to support my family for six months. I packed up my wife and baby, and we departed for Florida. I told her we were going to park in Fort Lauderdale for a month; I was going to fish off the dock, think about my career, and decide what I wanted to do next. It was going to be great, I said, nothing to do but lie in the sun and fish for one solid month.

We arrived in Fort Lauderdale, and I began to fish. Before the first week had passed, I was going nuts. I knew a life of sitting on the dock in the sun was not for me.

I called my father. "Dad," I said, "did you decide to go ahead and take that Kresge's location?"

He practically sputtered into the phone: "Boy, you sure are stubborn. I don't know how many times I have to tell you, you can't pay a thousand bucks rent and make money!"

That was what I expected him to say. "I'll tell you what," I offered. "If you'll sell me those two stores and give me three years to pay, I'll buy them. You might as well sell them to me, because this is the best deal you'll ever have to get rid of them. You know they're not going anyplace."

There was a short pause on the other end of the line: "Son, you just bought yourself two drugstores."

That was in 1948. I packed up my fishing pole and my family and headed north. When I got to Jamestown, I bought the old Kresge's lease, closed the old stores, and set up the operation my way. That store was very profitable almost from the beginning, and a few years later would provide the original investment from which the 1,700-store Eckerd Drugs chain began in Florida.

The point is not that I had more drugstore savvy than my father—far from it. In fact, when he died, many years later, at the age of ninety-four, I think he *still* thought he was right! Eckerds are stubborn that way. The point is that the drugstore business was changing; fundamental shifts were occurring in the buying habits of the whole country, and as a result the rules of the game were being rewritten.

For an eager young entrepreneur, willing to try new things, the climate was ideal. In the building of a big business, a critical element always is timing, that right combination of events and conditions, most of which are beyond the control of the players themselves. Some people call it fate; some say it's in the stars; I have come to understand it as the hand of the Lord. But however one explains it, timing is everything.

For the next twenty years, I poured all my energy into the challenge of building a drugstore empire. I can't take credit for it, but one thing is clear: the timing was perfect.

4

It is often said that new trends in the American pop culture start in California and gradually work their way eastward. Today's hot new West Coast idea often becomes part of tomorrow's Middle American mainstream.

For instance, in retail merchandising, the hot new idea that swept postwar America was the concept of "self-service," and it typically appeared in California before taking hold in the rest of the country. Some people have described me as being a pioneer in the conversion of drugstores from a full-service to self-service industry, but that "pioneer" label considerably overstates my role. At most, I helped accelerate the spread of what was already a growing trend in California.

Before World War II, the dominant force in American retailing had always been the small, full-service store, operated by a local owner-proprietor. Groceries, hardware, clothing, pharmaceutical supplies—every category of goods was marketed in this fashion. Retail stores served local communities. The shop owner lived in the community and was a neighbor to his customers. Services such as credit and home delivery were provided as a natural part of these personal relationships.

The profusion of competing brands that we know today did not exist, and consequently there was no need for massive national advertising campaigns. There were one or two kinds of a particular product, and the retailer stocked them. His customers came into the store, told him what they needed, and he got it for them. Credit was easier, because both parties knew each other. Home delivery was easier—and more necessary—because the customer lived nearby and quite often had no automobile, anyway. Price competition was less common, because the shopper had fewer options: soap was soap, and this is where you bought it. The merchant was expected to charge a fair price, and he usually did. It was a slower, more genteel way of doing business.

That pattern gradually changed as America became a more mobile society. People moved more frequently from place to place; an increasingly larger percentage migrated from small towns to the cities; the automobile allowed customers greater range in seeking goods. The upshot of all these changes was that shopping became an increasingly less personal affair. As it did, customers placed lower priority on the traditional services that the proprietor had provided. The emphasis shifted instead to price, convenience, and variety of selection.

As radio and television became fixtures in the American lifestyle, manufacturers gained direct access to every home, and advertising became a major force. Homemakers could now be urged to do their laundry with Duz, Whiz, Biz, or Sparkle, and when they came into the grocery stores to shop, commercial jingles still reverberated in their heads. Soap was no longer merely soap. They wanted to choose a particular *kind* of soap, and to do that they wanted to see and handle all the possibilities, which required more time and more shelf space.

To the merchant, that meant he had to provide bigger stores and more inventory. More importantly, perhaps, the consumers' increased mobility and lack of personal loyalty made retail merchandising more openly competitive; it was clear the public would shop wherever it could find the variety and convenience it was coming to expect—and at the best price.

These trends were well under way before World War II, and the enormous national upheaval of that war left the entire social landscape of American life permanently altered. The 10 million Americans who were in uniform came home to a different world. The incredible levels of energy and inventiveness that had been poured into the military effort were now redirected to civilian concerns, and the tempo of American life was permanently quickened.

The war was over, but the adrenaline stayed in the system. Factories that had geared up to produce tanks and planes now disgorged automobiles and washing machines at the same pace. Hometown boys who had been dispatched across the country or around the world stayed on the move, and society became more mobile. Individuals whose attitudes and expectations had been raised by their experiences in the war never regained their narrow perspectives. Rosie the Riveter stayed in the work force. The growth of new technologies, force-fed by military urgency, continued to multiply.

It was as if the normal forces of social change had been shifted into higher gear, and the future began arriving faster than any of us expected.

As I settled back into the routine of the drugstore business in Wilmington and Erie, in the late 1940s, I was vaguely aware that a fundamental shift was occurring in the way people shopped for the goods we were selling. Like many other businessmen of that time, it was not a thing which I understood intellectually, so much as it was something I sensed. It was less a matter of analysis and more a matter of intuition that told us things were changing. I began to sniff the air.

In the trade magazines and shoptalk among retailers, there was no shortage of new ideas, but one theme recurred: "self-service." The shift from full-service stores (in which clerks respond to individual requests from customers) to self-service (in which the customers select from a variety of goods, at their own pace, then pay at a checkout counter) met many of the growing demands for convenience, variety, and price. The transition occurred easily in the grocery business; by 1950, supermarkets were sprouting like mushrooms in suburban America, and the traditional full-service grocery store was rapidly becoming extinct.

For drugstores, however, that change had not yet occurred. The conventional wisdom of our industry was that people would not accept self-service in drugstores, that our products—medicines, drugs, and cosmetics—were more specialized and our customers depended too heavily on the advice of their pharmacists or cosmeticians to be comfortable making decisions for themselves in our stores. A potato is a potato, after all, and soap is soap, even if it is Duz-Whiz-Biz-Sparkle—but medicine is serious business, and people do not have the confidence to serve themselves in a drugstore.

All that sounds quite logical, but it turned out to be incorrect—or at least partially incorrect. As later developments proved, customers are bolder in making their own choices than was predicted. Given adequate information printed on the package and enough time to shop, people are not reluctant to select over-the-counter drugs for themselves.

Another development made self-service drugstores viable: the rapid expansion of the range of products which such stores sold. In the 1950s and 1960s, drugstores began to sell far more than just pharmaceuticals; we soon were doing major volume in such unrelated products as camera supplies, housewares, magazines and paperback books, and soft goods. The word *drugstore* itself might rightly be considered a misnomer today. In addition to drugs, the customer can expect to find everything from panty hose to charcoal grills—and neither product requires a physician's advice!

This is all hindsight, of course. At the time, it was generally thought that self-service merchandising would never work in the drugstore business. Not surprisingly, that premise was first challenged in California. I was reading a trade magazine one day and saw an article about a small drugstore chain in Los Angeles, which was successfully operating "pharmacy supermarkets." Soon afterward, I read another article about a merchant in the San Francisco Bay area, who was doing terrific business with self-service drugstores.

This was a totally new concept to me, and I decided to find out more about it. The only way I could be sure I was getting the whole story was to check it out for myself, so I bought an airline ticket and flew to California. I went first to Oakland, to visit one of the stores, called "PayLess Drugstore," which I had seen in the trade magazine. I had no appointment, no introduction; I just walked in the door like any other customer and cruised up and down the aisles. From the moment I entered the store, I was impressed with what I saw.

The place was full of people, most of them pushing carts, just like in a supermarket. The first thing that struck me was the variety of types of merchandise. I stood by the checkout counter—which was itself a thing I had never seen in a drugstore—and watched people buying cosmetics, candy, drugs, stationery, housewares, and all sorts of other things. It was amazing.

After watching for a while, I went to the back of the store, found the office area, and asked to speak to the manager. My luck was good; I met the gentleman who owned and operated the chain of six or seven PayLess stores, and he was extremely friendly and helpful. He welcomed me into his office, expressing shock that I had traveled all the way from Delaware to see his store. He was obviously proud of his operation; it was an innovative approach, and it was working, so he was like the proud papa at a christening. He beamed as he talked about it: "Anything you want to know," he exclaimed, throwing his arms out expansively, "just ask!"

So I asked. I virtually interrogated him. I asked about every aspect of the operation: gross profits, average volume per square foot, rent, advertising costs, payroll as a percentage of volume, merchandise mix, rate of inventory turnover, and so on. He didn't hold back a single scrap of information. The more he talked, the more I asked; and the more I asked, the more he answered; and when we were finished, we had spent a major part of the day, and I had a briefcase full of notes.

He was remarkably generous with his time and his information, and I took advantage of it. I had come to the right place. The next day, I visited another of his stores, in San Jose, and talked to the manager there. I also stopped people who were shopping, and if they were willing, interviewed them, standing in the middle of the aisles. "Why do you shop here?" I asked. I heard the same few answers over and over: "Because I can take my time, because people don't bother me there, because the prices are lower, because they have so much more stuff to choose from."

I left the Bay area after two days and went to Los Angeles. My target there was a chain of about a dozen stores that had introduced the self-service concept to southern California and was head-and-shoulders above every other drugstore operation in the area. My new Oakland friend had warned me that his L.A. counterpart might not be as receptive to my visit, and he was right.

When I arrived, I went straight to the closest store, wandered in, and started looking around. I must not have looked like an average casual shopper, because after I had been there a few minutes, the manager came up to where I was standing in an aisle and asked me what I was doing. I explained that I was in the drugstore business back in Delaware, had heard of his reputation, was in the area, and just stopped in to find out more about his store. "Well, go ahead," he said grudgingly, and brusquely returned to his office.

I went from there to the headquarters store and got in to see the owner of the chain. He received me with approximately the same warmth as his manager. He agreed to talk with me, and I made a big point of telling him I was on the East Coast and always intended to stay on the East Coast, thinking maybe his unfriendliness issued from paranoia about competition. But it didn't seem to make much difference. He was apparently unfriendly as a matter of principle.

One could hardly find greater contrast between two entrepreneurs than between the two I met in Oakland and Los Angeles. The L.A. owner had refined evasiveness to an art form. The more I asked, the less he told me. I tried telling him all my percentages back home, hoping it would make him less secretive, but I got nowhere. I finally gave up, thanked him for his time, and made a fast exit.

Although I was unable to get specific details of his business, it was obvious, in those and others of his L.A. stores I visited, that the self-service concept was working extremely well. The aisles were full of customers, the cash registers never stopped ringing, and the people whom I interviewed clearly preferred this type of shopping.

The L.A. stores themselves had great customer appeal. They were decorated all in white: white fixtures, white ceilings, white tile floors. A staff of young clerks roamed the aisles, carrying white feather dusters in their pockets, answering customers' questions, and being generally helpful.

One big feature of these stores was a special counter that sold nothing but ice-cream cones at three cents per cone. In every store, the ice-cream counter always had a line of customers. They would constantly wheel in big dollies with ten-gallon cans of ice cream. It was a perfect gimmick. The store made its own ice cream, at about a nickel a cone, I guessed, but it brought people into the store—adults, not children. They could be served fast; L.A.'s warm climate was right; there was not a lot of money tied up in inventory. I tried the same thing in my stores later, and it worked for me, too.

The trip to California showed me that what I had read in the trade magazines was not journalistic hype. It was real. In those drug-stores, self-service was alive and well. I visited other stores on that trip, conventional stores, and the contrast was vivid. In the conventional stores, things were quiet, slow. In the self-service stores, you could feel a different pulse; you could feel a sense of life and energy. It was obvious to me this was where the industry was headed. My biggest question—would people accept this kind of drug retailing?—had been emphatically answered: not only did they accept it, they loved it.

I had gone to California, in that winter of 1947, because I was restless for a change. I was looking for something that would yank me out of being just another drugstore owner; I was determined not to be ordinary. When I came back, I was sold on self-service. I was going to take a crack at it. I didn't know where; I didn't know how; but I was going to take a crack at it. The payoff, I figured, was going to be big for whoever got there first, back East. I was thinking maybe that could be me.

5

I returned to my stores in Delaware with the zeal of a new convert. My first impulse was naturally to try to sell to my family the idea of transforming our stores into the self-service format, but except for my nephew, who had been to California with me, I encountered a wall of skepticism.

The rest of my family responded to my tales of California as if I were Marco Polo returning from China—my stories were interesting, but what did it have to do with them? I can't blame them for their attitude; it was basic human nature. They were old hands in the drugstore business and not particularly open to change, especially not from a junior partner who knew a great deal less about it than they did. I tried to convince them it would work. Well, they said, maybe it works with those kooks out in California, but it will never work here.

I didn't try too hard to sell them, because I was so sure this was the wave of the future that it had to come. It was just too logical to miss, and I knew I was going to try it when I got my chance. The resistance of the Eckerd clan to the self-service concept was a combination of "It won't work" and the age-old wisdom of "If something ain't broke, don't fix it." Our drugstores were making good money the way they were. If they had been losing money, my father and brothers undoubtedly would have tried something new, but under the circumstances they saw no pressing need to do so.

So I tried to do what I could, by myself, to experiment with self-service. Unfortunately, the business climate in that area was not particularly hospitable to the new concept, at least not yet, and the implementation of the ideas I brought home with me was difficult and slow.

Over the next two years, I persistently sought ways to make the transition. I encountered difficulties and delays that I had not anticipated, but never during that time did I question that self-service was the way to go. I traveled to California for a second time, to gather more information, again taking with me Ed O'Herron, my nephew who was in the drugstore business in North Carolina. What we saw on that second trip confirmed my earlier impressions and made a believer of him. He returned to his home in Charlotte and put in a successful self-service drugstore that is profitable to this day.

An obvious strategy would have been simply to convert the existing drugstores that I owned to a self-service format, but they were all too small to make that possible. A self-service store requires much more floor space than a conventional store. As a rule of thumb, I like 10,000 square feet in one of our stores, and the conventional stores I owned at that time were only about 2,500. Instead of a small number of those old glass cases and high shelves on which merchandise is stacked, we needed lots of low, open shelf space and room for gondolas, which the customers could reach easily and browse in for themselves. We couldn't convert our stores to self-service, because they weren't large enough to allow any of that.

In 1949 my brothers agreed, and I finally had an opportunity to open the first self-service drugstore in Erie. There were four small Eckerd stores in Erie at the time, and I learned that a new supermarket was being planned at a good location on the perimeter of the city. We leased space on the strip adjacent to that supermarket and put in a large new store. Since we would be selling different merchandise and charging different prices from the four conventional Eckerd stores, we called this experimental one "QuikChek." The name was not very imaginative, but it did the job.

I ran an eight-page advertising supplement in the local newspaper to announce the opening of that store and nervously awaited the public response. When opening day came, we were all—even I, the most optimistic of the group—absolutely astounded at the flood of customers who poured into QuikChek.

As so often happens, our construction was behind schedule, and the parking lot had not even been paved yet, so it was a choking dust bowl all day. Fortunately it was summer—better dust than mud. Cars filled the parking lot and eventually began to block the highway in front of the store. We had to pull employees off their duty stations in the store to send them outside to direct traffic. It was an unbelievable success. When the dust had settled, we had registered more than double the highest sales volume of any weekend ever in any of our stores.

The success of that store whetted my appetite, but it also revealed one of the obstacles to my dream of mounting a major Eckerd self-service effort in that part of the country: having both conventional and self-service stores in the same town confused the customer. Even though we used the name QuikChek, we had frequent problems from people who knew it was an Eckerd-owned store. They would see a product advertised for the self-service store and try to buy it in one of the downtown stores. Or they could not understand why the price of the same products would be higher at the conventional stores. We tried to solve these problems with lines in our newspaper ads: ''This item not available at the following locations. . . ,'' but the confusion persisted, and we suffered some negative customer reaction as a result.

One conceivable solution would have been to operate the self-service stores under a completely different name, so that the customer would not know there was any connection at all, but to do so would eliminate many of the advantages of a multistore operation, especially the efficiency of combined advertising.

As we worked with that successful Erie QuikChek and continued to experiment with a modified self-service in a couple of other locations I became convinced that for self-service to work with optimal effect, I needed to go into an entirely new market area and start from scratch. The difficulties of mixing the old with the new were too great; what I needed was a fresh start in virgin territory.

For the next couple of years, as I tried to figure out where to go with this new concept, my mental map was pretty much confined to the major eastern metropolitan areas. The thought of moving to an entirely different region of the country did not immediately occur to me. I investigated the prospects in places like Baltimore, Philadelphia, and Washington, D. C., cities with which I was already familiar.

The problem was one of start-up cost. I did not have nearly enough money to sustain the kind of major advertising campaign that would be necessary to get a foothold in one of those cities. There were established local chains in every major city in the East—People's Drugs was in D. C., Sun-Ray in Philadelphia, and so on. To compete against them would require heavy advertising in the expensive metropolitan daily newspapers. That could be done, if I had owned enough stores to spread out the advertising costs, but I barely had enough money to start *one* store, let alone several, and it would be suicidal to go into those markets with a single store and no advertising.

Somewhere in this process, there began to rattle around randomly in my mind the possibility of striking out in a totally new direction, geographically. That idea had an additional appeal: in another part of the country, I would not be competing with myself. I was so confident of being successful wherever I went that I hesitated to open new stores in towns where the family already operated. We knew better than to feed on our own businesses, and that had happened to some degree, we suspected, in Erie with the QuikChek. I wanted to take customers away from somebody else, not from myself.

6

One dreary winter day, in March of 1952, as I worked at my little office in the back of the downtown store in Wilmington, I received a telegram. It was not even a personal telegram; it came from a realtor I had never met, and it obviously was one of those "Dear Druggist" telegrams that had been delivered to a large list of people.

But this particular telegram, on this particular cold, grubby day, hit a responsive spot somewhere in me. It advertised a business opportunity: "For sale, *cheap,* three self-service drugstores, Tampa Bay area, Florida." I looked out the window at the snow and the gray sky. I hadn't seen the sun for about a week. I had been working hard and was looking for an excuse to get away for a couple of days. The timing was right.

When I got off the plane in Tampa, the weather was so nice I figured it had been worth the trip, even if nothing came of the drugstore deal. I checked into the Floridian, an old downtown hotel, and called the realtor, a bright, aggressive woman named Helen Potusek. She came to pick me up and filled me in on the situation as we drove to see the stores.

The three stores were self-service drugstores—two in Tampa, one in the nearby beach town of Clearwater—operating under the name of "PayLess Drugstores." They were owned by a man named Frank

Berlin, who had been a successful retail druggist, who had lost interest in the new retail concept, now lived in California, and had become involved in the growing new plastics industry. Though he had a home in Florida, he was rarely in the state, almost never in the Tampa area, and had neither time nor inclination to worry about these struggling drugstores. He was ready to get what money he could from the stores and get out.

The stores themselves showed the negative effect of absentee ownership. Though they were attractive, clean, and well-kept, it seemed that they were not being managed especially well; they were losing money, and the situation was worsening. Inside, they were laid out like self-service stores, and I felt that two of the three had reasonably good potential to rebound. All they lacked was customers.

The most attractive aspect of the situation was that Frank Berlin was ready to cut a good deal. He wanted a buyer who would make an all-or-none offer—buy the stores, leases, fixtures, cash registers, inventory, everything in a single transaction. Cash up front. No percentages, no payout over a period of time. Just a straight cash deal, all or nothing.

I looked the stores over and told Helen I would buy two of the stores, the one in Clearwater and the suburban Tampa store, but that the one in downtown Tampa would always be a loser, and I would not buy it. She told me Berlin would not even discuss breaking up the package. "He will negotiate the price," she said, "but not the package," so if a deal was to be made, it would have to include all three stores.

From the numbers Helen was tentatively throwing around, I knew that this had the potential of being an unbelievably good bargain. I told her I was a serious buyer, and if she could get Berlin's numbers down a bit, we might be able to make a deal. On the plane back to Delaware, the more I thought about it, the more I felt this might be the time and the place. I called Helen from Wilmington and told her I intended to get a good Tampa attorney to conduct the negotiations. "Let's get Mr. Berlin to sit down with my attorney," I said, "and see if they can put together a deal." I was itching to go.

The attorney I retained for that original negotiation was a wily old cracker lawyer named Rex Farrior. Farrior was recommended to me by a mutual friend; he was one of the most highly respected attorneys in the state and without doubt one of the smartest. After I moved to Florida, he became one of my best friends and served as my personal counsel until his retirement.

Frank Berlin came to Tampa, from his vacation home in Sarasota, and Farrior cornered him and put together a tentative contract. The sticking point, which almost torpedoed the whole negotiation, was the value of the existing stock in the stores. Berlin agreed to sell me the stores with nothing paid for goodwill, nothing paid for fixtures, but I would have to buy all the inventory at his cost. That sounded reasonable on the face of it, but I explained to Farrior that I could wind up paying tens of thousands of dollars for a bunch of junk.

The stock on the shelves of those three stores was, to put it generously, ill-chosen. Berlin was so infatuated with plastics that he had loaded his drugstores with all kinds of plastic stuff—plastic mixing bowls, wash buckets, you name it—if they could make it out of plastic, it was there. It was all over the place, and I knew I would have to practically give most of it away the minute I moved in. Our deal almost died on the question of how to price the inventory, but Farrior finally persuaded Berlin to agree to a compromise: Berlin and I would come to Tampa, and the two of us would personally go to all three stores with a third party, who would price the inventory. I would have the right, within reason, to reject anything on the shelves that I thought was not marketable. The plastic goods that I kept, I would buy at half price. For anything else, I would pay full price.

The deal was made.

The next question was where I was going to get the money.

We had arrived at a final price of $150,000, which had to be paid immediately in cash. It was time to make another phone call to my older half-brother, not very different from the one I had made twenty years earlier, when I had a busted prop in Saint Louis. This time I called Ken, and I needed not $100 but $150,000.

Ken was a prosperous bachelor with lots of cash and a big heart. He had lived in the same apartment in downtown Erie for forty years, and that was where I went to tell him about the Florida opportunity. Ken enjoyed the good life; he owned a sailboat that he kept at Lake Erie, had lots of friends, and gave very little attention to the day-to-day operation of his drugstores. He relied on good managers and, in his partnership with his brother Bill, generally letting Bill make the decisions.

Ken was not a miser. He was generous with other people, but when it came to himself personally, he never saw a need to spend any money. I used to go into his apartment and say, "Ken, for heaven's sake, why don't you put some new carpet in here?" He would yell back at me, "For what? This is perfectly good carpet! And how do I know how much longer I'll be around?" (He was then approaching seventy; he died at the age of ninety-four.)

One thing Ken cared about deeply was the family reputation and the Eckerd name. He liked the idea of our being a successful drug-store clan, and as I told him about my deal in Florida I shared my conviction that this was a great opportunity to introduce self-service to a new area. It could eventually put us ahead of the pack here in the East, I predicted, and he liked that idea a lot.

I was not asking Ken for a handout. I owned the drugstore in Jamestown, fifty miles from Erie, which I had started in that old Kresge's location, after buying my father's two small stores. My Jamestown store was a very profitable operation; Ken knew the store well. The net worth of that store's physical assets alone was almost exactly $150,000. The deal I offered Ken was this: if he would give me the $150,000 cash, I would close the deal in Florida, and he would own a full fifty percent partnership in both operations.

Ken agreed to put up the money; he was easy to sell. He liked the idea of growth and doing something new, and he believed I would make money for both of us. As for me, the advantages of the arrangement were obvious: I could get started in Florida, and I would have the perfect partner, the kind who would put up the money and trust me to make it work.

It was the best deal either of us would ever make.

With Ken's money, I was ready to sign the contracts and begin my long-anticipated entry into the self-service drugstore business. When I went back down to Tampa to do the final paperwork and close the deal, I stayed once again at the old Floridian Hotel, in downtown Tampa, right across the street from one of the stores—the one I intended to close.

That was before the days of air conditioning, and the guest rooms in the Floridian were cooled by those old-fashioned, wood-bladed ceiling fans. I am not much of a sentimentalist, but many years later, when the Floridian put in an air conditioning system, I bought three of those fans and put them in my house. They are still there. I would like to think that I made that purchase strictly as a matter of business. Those are very good fans. After all, nothing works quite so well or so long as those old ceiling fans.

So just for the record, that is why I bought them. Strictly business. It had nothing whatever to do with sentimentality or nostalgia or the fact that it was that trip to the Floridian in 1952 that totally, permanently changed the course of my life. I bought those fans because I needed them, and they were available at a good price—I just want to get that on the record.

7

For the next few years, I shuttled back and forth between Wilmington and Florida, trying to keep my drugstores going up North while I built for the future in the South.

It would make a better story, I suppose, if I could report that the Florida business ignited immediately, but it didn't happen that way. Eventually, the growth in Florida would be explosive; we would reach a period when new Eckerd Drugstores seemed to multiply almost spontaneously. But that did not come in the first few years.

As in so many new ventures, the first few steps were the most difficult. I was a total stranger in the Tampa Bay area and relatively new even to the self-service style of drugstore management. I had two struggling drugstores—we closed the third one soon after buying it, as we expected—and a lot to learn. My challenge was to learn my lessons fast, keep the stores in the East profitable meanwhile, and begin making the contacts and laying the foundation for major expansion in Florida when the time came. All that added up to more than just a job—it was practically an obsession, taking all my time and attention.

One of the casualties of that period was my marriage. There were problems in our marriage almost from the beginning, and my prolonged absence during the war had made them worse. We came mutually to understand that we were not well matched, and in the postwar years I ignored the stress in our marriage by focusing on my work—

my business kept me on the road much of the time, and being gone was one way to deal with the conflict. Problems in a marriage are not really solved that way, unfortunately, and ours were no exception.

The issue that finally precipitated the divorce was an argument about what schools our children—we had a son and a daughter—should attend. My wife was a devout Catholic and felt strongly that our two children should be raised in the Catholic tradition. I approved heartily of their church activity but, when it came to their education, that was a different matter.

In Wilmington, the public schools happened to be excellent, due primarily to the commitment of the DuPont family to provide a quality educational system for the children of their employees in that city. I thought it fine for my children to go to the Catholic church; I called myself a Methodist, but I really had no interest in religion at all. But the Catholic schools they would have attended had no gymnasium, no library, and teachers who in my opinion, although dedicated, were not as qualified as those in the public schools.

I said no to Catholic schools, and my wife and I locked horns. The ensuing argument was the final blow to our already faltering marriage. My wife felt that my opposition on this point was part of an effort to wean the children away from Catholicism, whereas I felt that I was just trying to get them a good basic education. But in the aftermath of that dispute, without rancor or bitterness on either side, we decided to call it quits. We were actually burying a marriage that had gradually died.

Looking back, I can see that I probably neglected my family in those early days. If there is blame to be assessed, I will take my full share. But looking back is a pastime in which I rarely engage; a person can't spend his time wringing his hands over the past. I moved on.

In Florida, there were decisions to be made. I spent several days reviewing the operation with Frank Berlin's general manager and decided to retain him in that position, at least for the time being. I disliked the name "PayLess Drugstores," but realized it was well established with customers, so decided to operate under that name initially. I was eager to get the name *Eckerd* on my stores—and so was my brother Ken—but felt I should move slowly with that transition.

The surviving Tampa store was on Nebraska Avenue, outside the downtown area, and was doing a gross volume of about $1,500 a week. (It is still a very successful store, now grossing over $40,000 a week.) I established my office in the back of that store, on a little balcony overlooking the shopping floor. I spent almost half my time in Florida, and when I was there, I would go into my little office by 7:00 A.M. and work, either there or in the stores, until 10:00 or 11:00 P.M.

My life was all business—no sailing, no golf, no trips to the beach. When I was back in Wilmington and would see friends there, they would sometimes comment that they had not seen much of me. "Where have you been lately, Jack?" they wondered. "Florida," I would tell them. "Oh, yeah," they would respond. "You've got that tax deal down in Florida!" Many of them assumed that my Florida drugstores were nothing more than my excuse to spend time vacationing in the sun and write it off my income taxes as a business trip! Little did they know. I never saw the beaches; I could just as well have been in Antarctica for all the golf I played. I wasn't dodging taxes, I was building a drugstore chain; things were starting slowly, and I was fighting to stay alive.

As I began implementing new ideas in those two stores a set of policies and guidelines evolved that would remain basically unchanged throughout the growth of the Eckerd chain. Some of these were fundamental and very simple—such as a heavy emphasis on newspaper advertising. The advertising rate in the major daily newspapers, the Tampa *Tribune* and the St. Petersburg *Times,* was only eighty cents a column inch, and those papers reached the entire metropolitan area. At first I could afford only small, two-column ads, but I began running them regularly, advertising low prices and wide selections. For many years, as we expanded into new stores, our rule was that we would not operate outside the geographic area served by those newspapers, so all our stores could ride on a single advertising budget.

Another small but important decision was the floor layout of the stores themselves. That seems obvious now, but the big debate then was whether the aisles in the new self-service design should run from the checkout counters to the back of the stores, or across the stores sideways. The stores I bought were laid out crosswise, but I decided to copy the layout I had seen in California. Women were already accustomed to that pattern in supermarket: enter, go to the right, and work your way around the store counterclockwise, ending at the cash registers. We put our pharmacy departments in the back of the store, making it necessary for customers with prescriptions to walk past all the attractive merchandise on the gondolas.

Some things in the California model I changed. I felt, for example, that the typical customer, though obviously ready for self-service with most types of merchandise, still wanted help with cosmetics, and I put a full-service cosmetics counter in the stores. Most women like having a knowledgeable saleslady to give them advice and opinions on what looks best on their skin or works best on their hair. That is one area where the shopper does not want to be left alone, but unfortunately, the typical store does not have enough personnel to provide much help.

We had only about a dozen employees in those two stores, and they were naturally apprehensive about their new Yankee boss. They learned soon that I wasn't afraid to get in and get my hands dirty working with them. They also learned to expect me to walk in at any time, unannounced; they never knew whether I was in Florida or Delaware. I have always been a big believer in a personal, hands-on management style. Even after we became a major corporation, with stores all over Florida, I enjoyed and spent much of my time working on the front lines of the retail operation.

One day, several months after the change of ownership, I walked into the Tampa store and saw that the gondolas were still pointing sideways, though I had told the manager to move them to run the other direction. I asked the druggist where the manager was and was told he was taking the afternoon off. I said to the druggist, "Dr. Mosel, I've been trying to get Mr. Barry to turn these gondolas around, but somehow he hasn't gotten around to it."

"Well," said the druggist, trying to explain for his manager, "maybe it's that we don't have too much help around here."

"I appreciate that," I replied. "But why don't you and I take a crack at it?"

I was a middle-aged man, and he was quite a bit older, but the druggist's eyes sparkled at that: "You bet, Mr. Eckerd!" We took off our suitcoats, rummaged around in the stockroom, found some pipe and a crowbar, and during the rest of the afternoon, between the occasional customer who came in, turned around every gondola in the store.

At the end of 1952, we needed to "take inventory" in that annual ritual that all retailers endured in the days before computerized inventory control. The process required manually counting and logging every item on the shelves. Rather than close the stores during the week, as was usually done, I asked my employees to come in on New Year's Day to take inventory. I'm not foolish enough to think they actually enjoyed it, but I do believe it helped when they arrived at the store and saw me there, shirt sleeves rolled up, ready to work with them.

We worked hard all day, and when dinnertime came, I sent out to a nearby Spanish restaurant and brought back a big tub of yellow rice and chicken. We all sat back in the stockroom, on boxes, and ate and swapped stories, before going back to work. The employees didn't gripe a bit about having to work on a holiday; we all did it together and made a party of it. There were many occasions like that.

On the whole, my people were unusually loyal. Some of the original employees, when I bought the stores in 1952, stayed with me until they retired, many years later. I have always believed that a retail business's best asset is the people who meet the public every day—in our case that was the cashiers, druggists, cosmeticians, clerks, store managers, and assistant managers. I expected a lot from them, but I reciprocated with bonuses and then with stock options, and many of the early Eckerd employees benefited richly from the growth of our company in later years.

My game plan in Florida was to rebuild the two PayLess stores to a level of high profitability then use the money from those stores to open new locations around the Bay area. I had very little capital for expansion; the original $150,000 I had acquired from Ken was all I intended to get from that source. If we were to grow, it had to be slowly at first, one store at a time, using the profits from one store to open the next, and so on.

For the first two years, we actually lost money on the total Florida business. The lease on the downtown Tampa store ran for another year after we bought it, so that was a liability we had to cover. I used all the available cash flow to begin a total restocking of the other two stores, and that further slowed our progress toward expansion.

The Clearwater store itself was unfit for conversion to self-service. It broke all the rules for a profitable self-service operation: it was too small, only 2,000 square feet; and it was in a downtown location, which by the 1950s was usually fatal. I didn't think that store had a chance to survive over the long term, but somehow it was miraculously showing a profit, so we decided to keep it open as long as the bottom line was good. In those first two or three years, we needed every dollar of profit we could get, whether or not the store fit our overall profile.

After two years, the Florida business as a whole broke into the black, and after three years it was generating enough cash that we were able to expand to a third store. I had spotted what seemed to be a good location, on Henderson Boulevard in Tampa, next to a B & B Supermarket. The floor space was less than I wanted, but I was betting that some of the smaller shops around it would close and more space would become available, which it did.

We tied up the lease, and I went to a bank in Clearwater to try to borrow the money. This was one of the best tests of the strength of our business: would a bank be willing to lend us money to expand to a new location, based on the track record of the existing stores? It turned out to be easy. The bank approved the loan with no delay, and we soon opened at the Henderson Boulevard location.

It was a small beginning, but it was at least a beginning. The important thing was that we had turned around the original two stores, begun to expand, and were making money. Perhaps even more important is that I was gradually learning what to do. It had taken me three years to add one store. In the next three years, I would add two more stores. And then we would shoot for the moon.

8

Rex Farrior

Rex Farrior was a senior partner in the law firm of Shackleford, Farrior, Stallings, and Evans until his retirement in 1974. He is still bright and active at the age of ninety. He goes daily to his downtown office and enjoys his status as the elder statesman of the Tampa legal community.

One day in 1952 a realtor named Rogers from Clearwater and his lady associate named Potusek walked into my office. They said, ''Mr. Farrior, we have a listing of three rundown drugstores. We have a buyer, willing and able to buy, but we can't get a contract out of the man who owns the property. We give up.'' Those were practically their exact words.

So I called the man, a man named Berlin, and he came to town and stayed over at the Floridian Hotel. I went to his room at the hotel, and we negotiated all day long, until about six. We had almost come to an agreement, but when I went back the next morning, we had to start over. I did that for about four days. On the fourth day, I had a contract that I thought was our maximum offer and I thought he would take. In the meantime, I had come to the conclusion the man must be broke. He was trying to salvage something from those stores, that's all.

On the fourth day, about five, he signed. The buyer had to place $150,000 in escrow with my law firm until we had paid off all the outstanding bills and had complied with the Florida law to clear all the claims against those stores. We didn't know how much Mr. Berlin owed. After the bills were paid, he kept what was left. I remember every detail except how much he got, but I recall it wasn't much. By the time we paid all the bills and delivered those stores free and clear, the money was about gone.

I first met Jack Eckerd when we closed the sale. He came down from up north to close. I remember he shut down one of those stores because it was unprofitable. One thing about Jack Eckerd: he never kept a store open that didn't produce. And any man that didn't produce, he just disappeared. One example was when he had about twenty stores. I was on Jack's board then, and he had a comptroller working for him. Once, when the board met, someone noticed that fellow wasn't around anymore and asked Jack about it. He said, "Well, it's not his fault that we outgrew him." That's the closest he ever came to telling us why he let someone go.

His first manager was a man transferred down from Erie. I was at his house one night with Jack, and they were talking about the drugstores. Jack was making some suggestions. Berry said, "Well, if I'm gonna have to do things that way, maybe I just oughta resign." Jack said, "That's a good idea, you are now resigned." That was the end of it.

9

As my business career began to heat up, there was a new development in my personal life, which was more important than what was happening in the banks or the drugstores or that little office on Nebraska Avenue. I fell in love with a lady from Tampa. At the age of forty-three, after having decided that I could be happily married only to a job, I was smitten like a lovestruck teenager.

That was in 1957; I met the former Ruth Binnicker in February, and we were married in March. We are still in love, as much today as ever.

I met Ruth as the result of the stratagems of Rex Farrior, my attorney, and his wife. I began to visit often with Rex and his wife, and they worried about my lack of female companionship. After the breakup of my first marriage, I had no interest in seeing women; I was too busy with my business.

But the Farriors thought I needed to "meet a nice girl," as they put it, so they arranged for me to meet Ruth, who was at that time a young widow with a family. From the first night we met, there was a special chemistry between us, and we were married less than two months later. We were both adults, and we knew who we were and what we were looking for in a mate. We were both serious-minded people, and we knew what we were doing.

Ruth Eckerd

Ruth Binnicker Eckerd is a small, gracious woman with a sense of style in dress and bearing. She speaks with the soft accent of old-fashioned southern gentility. She is a native of Tampa, the daughter of a prominent banker, and attended Florida State University.

Jack really did sweep me off my feet. I never intended to remarry, after the death of my first husband, who died of a heart attack when the children were ages two, six, and eight. I was a widow for two years. I felt that I would choose to spend the rest of my life without remarrying; I had children to raise, and I just could not imagine being interested in another man.

The Farriors set it up, of course. They were dear and old friends of my parents and me. I had known them all my life. Lera Farrior was an inveterate matchmaker; she got acquainted with Jack, and she couldn't stand seeing that tall, good-looking man drifting around on the beaches alone. So she called and asked me to see him. I think she was working on Jack more than she was me.

I did not want to go. It took some persuading, but because they were such good friends, I agreed. Still I didn't look forward to it. I was doing them a favor. We have a week-long social event in Tampa called "Gasparilla," rather like the Mardi Gras. The Farriors wanted me to go with Jack to the Tuesday night ball. Someone else had already asked me, and I had said, "No," so I felt I could not appear. So I went to the ball with my mother, met Jack, and we talked afterwards.

Jack asked me to go with him to another party on Thursday, but I had no one to stay with my children. Jack went on to the party with the Farriors, but later that night, he came to my house, and from then on we were together more than apart.

I was quite taken with him. He was, and is, a handsome man. That first time we met, I asked him what business he was in, and he said, "Drugstores." I wondered if he was a druggist. I really knew nothing at all about him.

Things were serious almost from the start. Jack is not the kind of person to enjoy just going out, or dating, or whatever you would call it. I sensed he was someone who really loved a family. I could tell that this man would not enter into a casual relationship at all; he was looking for a family and a home. I knew that this was something I was going to have to deal with in a serious way, and after I was with him a few times, I realized I was getting in pretty deep, too.

We were married about six weeks later. We met about February 10, and we were married on March 30.

Rex Farrior

Jack called me at the office one day and asked me to meet him for lunch—said he had something he wanted to talk with me about.

We met at a little restaurant at the corner of Polk and Tampa, a place where you could get lunch for fifty cents, including iced tea and dessert. Of course, that wasn't last year, either, so fifty cents meant a little more.

What Jack wanted to talk about was a woman he had met up north somewhere. He didn't seem all that excited about her, but that was what he wanted to talk about. I went home that night and told my wife, "Jack is a family man, and he's lonely without a wife. We need to find him a nice Tampa girl."

He met Ruth at the Gasparilla Ball one night, and he spent the night here in our guest room. A couple of days later, he went with my wife and me to a banquet at the Tampa Terrace Hotel, in the Palm Room. Jack left the table, and didn't come back for a while, so I went looking for him. He was in the lobby, talking on the phone to Ruth. He asked if I would take him out to her house, and I did. As I recall, he stayed 'til about two-thirty. I think they liked each other right off. They got married within two months.

10

I learned many of the lessons of those early years by trial and error.

It became obvious early that, for a self-service store to work, it would have to stock products that I knew nothing about. Plumbing supplies, for example. That was a line of merchandise for which my old-fashioned pharmacy background had not prepared me. I needed plumbing supplies in my stores, but nobody in my company knew how to buy and stock them.

I thought I had the answer. I found an elderly gentleman who had been in the plumbing business before he retired. I assigned him one gondola in a particular store and said to him, "I don't have any idea what to tell you to buy, but keep that gondola stocked with plumbing items." He did his best, but the whole project was a disaster. I probably lost $10,000 on that mistake. The kind of professional plumbing equipment he bought was not what our customers wanted. He stocked up with things like high-quality wrenches and plumber's tools, which nobody but a professional would buy. What we needed instead was inexpensive stuff: screwdrivers, simple tools, the kinds of things a housewife or a handyman would use. I know that now, but I didn't know it then. It was one of many expensive lessons I had to learn.

Another line of merchandise we began stocking was soft goods— simple items of clothing such as shirts, pants, and so on. How does a drugstore get into that? This time, I decided to contract the job out to a New York buyer, as many small businesses do. I consulted a directory of New York buyers, called two or three of them, and finally made a deal to have $10,000 to $12,000 of soft goods sent to our stores.

It was another catastrophe. When the first shipment of goods arrived, to our dismay, it consisted only of drab women's smocks. These buyers were sitting up in New York, ordering clothing for Florida, and they obviously had never consulted a weather report. So we had a load of smocks, priced at $4.98, which actually cost us $3.50, and we eventually ended up selling them for $.98 apiece.

To an old drugstore man like me, soft goods were a pain in the neck. I would be in a store, and my employees would unload a crate of women's panties and bring them up to me. "Mr. Eckerd, what do you want to sell these for?" Well, I didn't have the slightest idea.

"When you buy them, how much do you usually pay?" I asked.

"Well, Grants gets fifty-nine cents for them."

"Okay, mark them for fifty-four cents and put them out."

Not exactly a sophisticated approach to marketing, but that was the way we had to do it. I knew I needed to get into new lines of merchandise, and I had to experiment. There was no book to read on how to do this. It was the price I paid for ignorance and inexperience, which I gradually overcame. Fortunately, I made most of my mistakes on one or two stores, instead of several dozen. If I had had ten stores, I would have lost $100,000 instead of $10,000 on that plumbing deal!

The capacity to stock new types of merchandise was one of those double-edged aspects of the self-service stores: it was both a risk and an opportunity. In the case of unfamiliar products such as plumbing and soft goods, it was possible to lose money fast. But it also opened up the market to many new brands, and the manager who had a knack for picking popular new styles could get the edge on his competitors. It was another way in which self-service stores brought a more wide-open, volatile style of competition to the drugstore industry.

In conventional stores, managers could hardly afford to stock anything unless it was highly advertised, brand-name merchandise. There was limited shelf space, and it all was used for the few brands which the customer was most likely to request. In self-service stores, on the other hand, there was room to put out several brands of every item, allowing the customer to look them over. The store could take a chance on products from newer, smaller companies, which opened up a whole new area of merchandising not based strictly on brand-name popularity.

Everyone benefits from this new competitive openness. The customer gets a wider choice. The small manufacturer gets a chance to get his products into the marketplace. The retailer can make better deals with his suppliers, since he is not captive to the few major companies.

Another spin-off benefit to the retailer is that his total volume increases. A manager can take several dozen tubes of Colgate toothpaste and stack them up in the aisle, and for some reason will sell more toothpaste than if he puts only a few tubes out. That is not logical, but it always works that way. A big gondola of merchandise sells more than two or three spaces on a shelf. So the overall volume increases for the druggist who has the space to pile it higher and wider.

People buy on impulse, responding to the visual cue of a mass display. That is why you see displays in modern stores going bigger and bigger, higher and higher. The customer walks in and sees a huge mound of products and unconsciously says to himself, *Good grief, that must really be good stuff, if they think they're gonna sell that much of it!*

In such a situation, skill in the selection of inventory is obviously more important than in the days when a few major manufacturers dominated the industry.

Because of my plan to expand to new stores, I tried to develop a strategy for the selection of new locations. Over the next ten years, the choice of new sites for Eckerd stores would be the most important decisions I would make. (Actually, the most important decision in my life would come years later, but I didn't know that at the time.)

Choosing the ideal location for a new store will never be a science; it seems to involve a certain amount of intuition. But in a booming economy and rapid population growth such as we had in Florida in the 1950s and 1960s, with so many retail outfits expanding so rapidly, some of the fiercest competition in our business was the race to identify and control good locations. There were key characteristics we sought. First, we had to stay in the Tampa Bay area, in order to minimize our advertising costs. We would outgrow this rule eventually, of course, with Eckerd stores in fifteen states from New Jersey to Texas, but for the first few years we stayed at home.

Next, we looked for areas with the highest concentration of housing within a mile and a half—that was the greatest distance I figured the average housewife would travel to shop on a regular basis. Next, we looked for easy access from major thoroughfares, neighborhoods with diversity of age ranges, and the absence of other nearby shopping clusters. The trick was to spot the hot new shopping areas *before* they got hot and real estate costs correspondingly went through the roof.

The most important single element of our success in choosing locations was the practice of putting our stores adjacent to supermarkets in strip malls. Being next door to the right grocer was critical to a new drugstore. The grocer would bring women into his store twice a week; the druggist was lucky to get them twice a month. If the combination was right, it helped both stores; shoppers liked the convenience of being able to visit both stores in one stop.

Drugstore-supermarket combinations worked so well that new strip malls in the best locations were frequently built around them. Obviously, the supermarkets were larger and did a much higher dollar volume, so they were the dominant partners in these relationships. The big supermarket chains called the shots; they would tie up a prime location for one of their stores, then decide which drugstore to invite to build alongside them.

Unfortunately for us, in the fifties, the best and fastest-growing supermarket chain in Florida was Publix, which had an exclusive arrangement with a local chain called Touchton Drugs. It was a partnership nobody else could crack. Publix had a terrific real-estate department and plenty of money for expansion. They always seemed to grab a promising new location before anyone else spotted it, which meant that Touchton automatically got the rights to put in a drugstore there. Other drugstore owners, like me, tried to bid for some of the Publix action, but found them uninterested in shopping around for new partners. The heads of Publix were unusually loyal by nature, thought Touchton operated good stores, and were not interested in talking to anyone else.

In finding new sites, I avoided the big enclosed shopping malls almost as religiously as I avoided downtown locations. The huge new malls popping up all over Florida and the rest of the country were not good locations for drugstores, in my opinion. The malls were always dominated by two or three gigantic department stores, which drove the rent sky high for everyone else. High rent is acceptable to smaller stores that do little of their own advertising, because they depend on the big department stores to pull traffic into the malls. We did our own advertising and therefore didn't need that help, so we were better off in strip malls, where the rent was cheap and access easier.

We also discovered—once again through trial and error—that being in an enclosed mall was bad for our prescription business. The person who leaves a doctor's office with a prescription to be filled wants to get in and out fast, without the hassle of parking and going through a big shopping mall. Prescription buyers are not impulse shoppers, and we did less than half as much prescription business in mall stores as in strip stores, all other things being equal.

Once we had our original stores operating solidly in the black, expansion was constantly on my mind. The two indispensable ingredients of expansion were the ability to get the right locations and the ability to get the money. In each case, we had to have the confidence of other people—the supermarket owners in one case, and the bankers in the other. In both cases that confidence had to be earned. At first glance, it may seem that to move from two stores to five stores in six years is very slow growth, but this was not a business that rewarded impatience. The critical task of those years was to develop a track record that would inspire confidence, then the growth would come.

In the late 1950s, I did not have the confidence of local bankers. I didn't speak their language. I changed banks twice in the first four years; I would ask for more money, and they would tell me I was trying to move too fast. I couldn't even get the real-estate people to talk to me about the good locations, and I don't blame them. They didn't know me, and in a boom-town economy with a state full of hustlers, they were wise to be cautious.

The big grocery chains who owned strip centers wouldn't do business with me, but why should they? They sublet to drugstores on percentage leases, collecting a base rent against a percentage of the druggist's volume, so they wanted to rent to successful, high-volume drugstores. Why should they go with an unknown like me, when they could choose an established chain like Walgreen or Liggett—who had the additional advantage of having enough cash to outbid me on a deal?

I had to be patient and build credibility with landlords, suppliers, and banks. It took time.

Gradually, though, cracks appeared in the wall. The first opportunity I had to expand into a prime location came in 1959, when a terrific site in St. Petersburg unexpectedly became available to me. It was in a new shopping strip that was being built; I had already looked at the location and learned that Walgreen had tied it up and had eaten my heart out at being unable to compete with them for it.

For some reason, in the final stages of their negotiations, Walgreen decided to press the landlord over some small detail, and he got mad at them and canceled the deal. Someone had told him who I was, that I ran a good operation, and that I had been trying to find new drugstore locations. He called me and said, ''Do you want this lease?'' I said yes without a moment's hesitation. He said, ''How fast can you get over here and sign it?''

As good as that opportunity was, I had trouble borrowing money for the store. It was a large store, an expensive one, and I had to have the money quickly. The building was already built, ready for the fixtures. The landlord wanted me to close the deal within a week. When I went to my bank in Clearwater to borrow the money, I got a flat turndown. It didn't even make me mad. I just thought the banker was a fool; I'd find the money someplace else; the store would be a big success; and he'd be sorry. All of which happened just that way—except the part about the banker being sorry. I don't know if he was or not; I never took the time to find out.

The most crucial breakthrough in my business came in 1959, when I made my first deal with Publix.

It seems excessive, perhaps, to attach such significance to a single event, particularly one that occurred so early in the life of my company, but I honestly believe the first deal with Publix was of that magnitude.

We had five stores at the time. I received a phone call at home one night from Joe Blanton, head of the real-estate department at Publix. I had gotten acquainted with Joe, over the past few years, as a result of my many unsuccessful attempts to do business with Publix. He was calling from the Publix offices in Lakeland, about seventy-five miles away.

''Hey, Jack,'' he said, ''the old man wants to talk to you about some stores. Can you come over sometime tomorrow?''

''Not before seven in the morning!'' I answered, barely trying to hide my enthusiasm. We confirmed a meeting time for the two of us and ''the old man,'' who was George Jenkins, head of the hottest grocery chain in Florida.

Before we ended our phone conversation that night, I tried to learn how serious their interest might be, so I asked Joe, ''By the way, I'm curious, what's happened to Touchton?''

''Well, Jack, we just lost a friend.''

"What do you mean?" I thought maybe something had happened to Walt Touchton, the owner of the chain.

"They've decided to sell out to Liggett, and we don't much like Liggett's operation."

The next day, I went to Lakeland for the meeting, and with very little negotiation, George Jenkins offered me the same deal that Touchton had: we would do business together on a group of five locations they were planning, and if things worked out well with those stores, we would have the first call on any locations they opened up.

It was an invitation to the Big Time.

As with most big opportunities, however, there was a major hurdle to cross. I had to enter a joint agreement with them immediately for five stores: one in Tampa, one in Clearwater, and three in St. Pete. I asked if I could do just part of the package. "Let me take a look at those five locations and see which ones I want," I suggested.

"Oh no, we can't do that," Blanton emphatically responded. "We don't intend to run around dealing with a different drugstore at every location. We want to put the deal together with somebody who can handle the whole thing. Why don't you go look at the locations? If you like them, they're yours. If you don't like them— no problem, we'll find someone else."

I left Lakeland with plenty to think about on my drive back to Clearwater that morning. I had been trying to build with Publix for years, with no luck. I had even made it a practice to stop into their offices occasionally, just to tell them I was still around and still wanted to do business with them. Anytime I saw Joe Blanton, I would remind him, "I want to do business with you guys. I'm gonna live down here and expand down here, and you're the kind of people I want to work with." But they always had complete loyalty to Touchton, and it looked as if that partnership might never end. This offer was obviously a great opportunity.

On the other hand, I would have to jump from five stores to ten in one shot, and that would not be easy. I would have to find the money somewhere and would have to do double the volume I was already doing. It would be a quantum leap for me, and I had to be sure I knew what I was getting into.

I drove around that day and looked at the five locations. They all looked excellent, as I had expected; I was convinced all of them were winners. That settled it, from a strictly professional perspective. This was the opportunity I had worked for, and only a fool would turn it down.

From a personal point of view, however, it was a much closer call. I was married, and family life meant more to me now than it ever had before. I was forty-five years old and ambivalent about whether to try to shoot for the moon with my business. Until then, I had thought I might build up to eight or nine stores, making sufficient income to cover my family's needs, and then take it easy.

When that Publix offer came, it was decision time—a watershed in my life. There was no way to get into it gradually; it was literally a double-or-nothing decision. I also knew that those five new stores were just the beginning, that if I went from five to ten, I was going for everything.

Basically, I decided to bring Ruth into the decision process. I was ready to go, but not at the expense of my family. That night, I told her about it.

"Well, Babe," I began, "I finally cracked Publix," and I laid the whole deal out for her. She listened carefully and, though she wasn't excited about the idea, advised me to go for it.

There was still the problem of getting the money, but I was so confident the deal was golden that I couldn't imagine being rejected for a loan. I went to my bank in Tampa and explained what I wanted to do; I needed $750,000, five stores at $150,000 each. To my disbelief, the loan department turned me down cold. It was the same old story: I was moving too fast, they said, trying to expand from five to ten stores at one time. "How about $300,000 for two of them?" they asked, and if I did well, I could come back for more.

I explained that I couldn't do it, that this deal with Publix was five or nothing, but the answer was still no. I argued the point, showing them my profit record from my other stores, but to no avail.

I went home discouraged that night and told Ruth about the bank's refusal to lend me the money. My bank was the same bank where her father had been president and chairman of the board. He was already retired when I married Ruth, but he still kept a little office on the ninth floor of the First National Bank building. He was still sharp; he knew more about municipal bonds than practically anyone else in Florida.

"Why don't you go up and see Dad?" Ruth suggested that night. I said, "Well, he's not active, and I hate to bother him." But she insisted: "You ought to go to see him. He would like to know what's going on, anyway."

So the next day I went to his office and told him about being turned down for the loan. He listened patiently until I was through.

Then he spoke: "Yeah, Jack," he said, "I've already heard about it."

"They made a big mistake," I said glumly.

"I know that, too."

There was a long pause. There seemed to be very little left to say. "What would you do if you were me?" I asked finally.

He stood up at the window, looked down at the street, and pointed to the front doors of the Exchange National Bank Building, his bank's chief competitor, which was right down the street. "I would go down the street," he declared.

And I did. I rode down the elevator, crossed the street, entered the giant doors of the Exchange Bank, and that same afternoon I had my $750,000.

The deal with Publix turned out to be more significant than even I had dared to dream. It ignited the spectacular growth of my company, which continued for the next sixteen years. In addition to the five new stores, I contracted with Publix to build a new office building and warehouse for me in Tampa, to accommodate the growth that I knew was coming. We opened each of the five stores on schedule, and they all were big profit makers. Before those were finished, we already had more on the drawing boards, and ultimately Eckerd Drugs and Publix built over 150 supermarket-drugstore combinations.

From the time I decided with Ruth to accept the Publix offer, I was 100 percent confident that it would be successful. I felt I had a handle on how to manage self-service stores. We had good locations and super personnel, from top to bottom. The Publix track record was proven. The expansion would cut my advertising costs in half, cut general management costs, and enable me to make better deals with my suppliers. I literally would have bet my life on it.

Why did my Tampa bank not see it that way? I can only guess that they were afraid to stick their necks out. They were into something they did not understand—retail merchandising—and instead of getting someone in their loan department who knew something about it and could interpret my figures, they just played it safe.

I've often wondered why Publix took a chance on me, why they didn't go with a bigger chain, like Walgreens. One factor was that they were a Florida business and preferred not to work with out-of-state companies, all other things being equal. My figures also looked pretty good. But the best explanation, I think, is that the people at Publix, after they looked at all the statistics and analyzed all the numbers, were hunch players. They trusted their intuition. Somehow they had a hunch that I was worth betting on.

I'm glad they played their hunch, and I'm especially glad they turned out to be right.

Since that time, I have made bigger deals on at least eight or ten different occasions, and have thought very little about it. We once bought thirteen stores in Atlanta in a single transaction. Those were bigger deals than the Publix offer in absolute dollar terms, but in terms of my life, there was never another deal nearly as big as this one.

Ruth Eckerd

Jack has always been wonderfully considerate about major deci-sions that would affect our family life. He always consults me about anything big. When he got that call from Publix, the first thing he did was to come home to discuss it with me. I remember what he told me: "If I do this, the business can get real big, but I'm not sure that's what we want. This is going to make a difference in our lives. Instead of having a handful of drugstores, we could wind up having an entirely different life."

He knew the business would take off if he made the deal, and he knew there was a price to pay. He explained it, and then he asked me, "What do you think?"

I knew him well enough to know he wasn't going to be happy with the few stores he had. He talked about taking it easy, but I noticed that even when he had excuses to play, he didn't take them. He needed a challenge. I felt this was what he was good at, and he was anxious to do it, so I was for it.

I think I remember what I said: "As far as I'm personally con-cerned," I told him, "and as far as the children are concerned, maybe you ought to go slow. But I think I know you well enough, and I don't think you'll ever be happy or satisfied if you do. So I think you'd better sign those leases."

That was a major turning point. He had a wonderful mind and a discipline to achieve, and they had to come out in some way. He definitely needed a challenge. At one time he had wanted to be an airline pilot, and I've often thought that if he'd stayed in aviation, he would have owned an airline by now.

He told me that on a trip to Florida once, he thought about people needing a place to stay. This was before the days of motels, and people had to stay in little roadside cabins or in downtown hotels in these little towns; and they were generally awful. It occurred to Jack that there could be a chain of motels strung out along the road, places that would have a reputation for being clean and comfortable.

That was the Holiday Inn model, right there, long before anyone ever heard of a motel chain. Jack is the kind of person who could have put something like that together.

He sincerely sought my input on the Publix decision. It was one we had to make together; he was not asking me just to make me feel good. I do believe if I had said no at that time, he would not have done it.

Did it change things? Oh yes, it did. After the Publix deal, he worked terribly hard, long hours. He tried to come home for dinner every night, but he would bring home boxes full of work—not just a briefcase, but literally big boxes of invoices and things he worked on until late every night. He worked almost every Saturday. He drove himself, but then he always has. There was no way he could go by one of his stores without going in, checking on things, talking to the employees. That is the reason the chain has been so successful; he was such a driving force.

Yes, it did change our lives. But it has been worth it. Definitely.

11

One of the battles we had in the early days of Eckerd Drugs was fought in the courtroom.

In those days, the state of Florida had on its books something called the "Fair Trade Law." No legal statute was ever less accurately labeled than that one. In my opinion, it should have been called the "Unfair Trade Law." This peculiar law prohibited a retail merchant from cutting the price of a product below that charged by any other merchant in the state.

The law was absolutely absurd. I don't know how it ever got past the legislature. What it amounted to was legalized price fixing between manufacturers and large retailers. A big company like Colgate-Palmolive, for example, would sign a contract with a Florida store to sell a bottle of shampoo for fifty cents. According to the so-called Fair Trade Law, it was then illegal for any other store to offer the bottle of shampoo to its customers for *forty-five* cents!

The effect of the law was to virtually eliminate discount retail stores. Strange, but true. The rationale of the law was that it protected small retailers from giant chains, which could presumably cut prices and get all the business. But in the real marketplace, it did just the opposite.

Its result was that new small companies like mine couldn't use price cutting as a way to get a foothold in established markets. The only way for us to get new business was to cut prices, which we could do, since we were strictly cash-and-carry, with no charge accounts, delivery, or other nonessentials, which most of our large competitors had adopted. My strategy was to run a lean, no-frills operation and pass the savings on to the customer—but how could I do that if the law forced me to charge the same prices as the full-service stores and well-established chains?

The law made no sense. I was convinced it was unconstitutional, so I decided not to comply with it. From the time I moved to Florida, I cut prices on various products, whenever I felt it was good business to do so. I figured I was so small I could probably get away with it, and for a while I was right. But as my business grew and my ads became larger and more numerous, my competitors began to notice me.

Two different manufacturers came down on me at the same time: General Electric, who had a popular little steam iron, and Miles Laboratories, maker of Alka-Seltzer. I was cutting prices on these items, and the two companies decided to stop me. First they merely called to warn me: stop discounting our goods, they said, or we will sue. I ignored them.

After three such calls, I got a visit from an attorney representing the two companies. "From now on," he told me, "we're playing for keeps. If you do this one more time, we're going to haul you into court."

At that point, I called Rex Farrior and told him what was happening. "Okay, Rex," I said, "if they put me in jail, are you gonna get me out?"

He laughed: "You keep on cutting prices, Jack, and let them sue you. I think I can beat them."

So that's what I did. Rex was a great trial lawyer, and I trusted his advice. I ran another set of ads with discount prices on those same products, and the manufacturers, true to their threat, filed suit. Rex got an early scheduling of the case and went into court to argue that the law was unconstitutional.

Rex Farrior

I took a phone call from Jack one day. He told me he was calling from his store out on Nebraska Avenue. He said, "Rex, there's a lawyer out here that says that if I don't quit cutting prices on Alka-Seltzer and G. E. Steam Irons, he's gonna sue me. I bought this stuff; it's mine, and I think I oughta be able to sell it for whatever I want."

I told him I agreed with him. I had never actually read the law, but I looked it up and decided Jack was right. In my research, I learned that during the Depression, about 1933, the state of California had passed this so-called Fair Trade Law, which said that if one retailer signed a contract with a manufacturer to sell a brand-name product at a certain price, no retailer could sell it at a lower price. Lots of states copied that law from California in the thirties, and Florida was one of them.

The law was still on the books because small, independent stores couldn't afford a lawsuit. They couldn't spend the money to fight the big companies; it just wasn't worth it, so they complied with the law. But Jack wasn't that kind of man. He thought it was unfair, and he was gonna fight it.

Fortunately, our case was heard before a good judge who knew the law and went by the law. It doesn't always work that way. His name was Harry N. Sandler, a judge in the circuit court of Hillsborough County. We won the suit. Judge Sandler wrote an order declaring that clause to be unconstitutional as a price-fixing act. Which it was, nothing else.

The companies appealed the decision right up to the Supreme Court of the state of Florida. On the appeal, Jack offered me this deal: if we lost, I would get nothing; if we won the appeal, he would pay me $10,000, which was a lot of money back then.

Needless to say, we won, on a unanimous ruling by the Supreme Court. (Judge Glenn Terrell wrote the opinion—he was a student of the law and quite a philosopher.) So the final result was that the law was ruled void, and Jack could cut prices on anything he wanted. It was quite a victory, not just for Jack, but for all the small retail stores that were trying to get started in those days.

That law was unjust, so he fought it and won. I think that typifies the character of the man.

When that case went to the Florida Supreme Court, I was not able to go to the trial, but I heard about the masterful job Rex did on those company lawyers. The way I heard it, he was merciless. They had their whole battery of attorneys there against him, and he was just an old cracker lawyer, all by himself. So he said, "Here's these New York lawyers, these high-priced guys from up north, coming down here representing those big New York companies, and I got a little client down here with a few drugstores, and all he wants to do is save the people of Florida some money.

"He knows there are lots of people in Florida who can't afford all those services. They can't afford to have things delivered to their door. They just need medicine at a low price. Now are you gonna let these New York lawyers come down here and tell him he can't save these poor Florida folks that money?"

Rex won that case with a unanimous judgment by the court, and that was the end of the Fair Trade Law.

Beating that law was one of the biggest things that ever happened to me. It put Eckerd drugstores into orbit. I got publicity all over the state, the kind of free advertising money can't buy. The case, and the attention it received, created an image for me and my stores as the champion of the little man. The whole thing was played in the Florida media as a David-and-Goliath story—the small businessman who took on the big companies and won, defending his right to give the public lower prices. There is no way to put a value on that kind of public exposure, and it came at a perfect time to give momentum to our growing business.

At that point in my life, I appeared to have everything going for me. But in the things that mattered most, all was not well. Professionally, I was on a winning streak, and I was too consumed by the excitement of Big Business to realize I was building my entire life on what would prove to be a faulty foundation—a foundation of personal pride and ego satisfaction. I was a fool. I plunged through life on the premise that I could construct a world in which all my needs would be met. It was a faulty premise, and eventually I would be forced to confront it.

Eckerd drugstore in Wilmington, Delaware, 1946.

Jack Eckerd's first drugstore in Jamestown, New York, 1937.

Above: Groundbreaking of an
Eckerd drugstore, 1957.

Right: Jack Eckerd and Harry
Roberts, first Eckerd drugstore
president after Jack Eckerd, 1960.

Left: Governor Ronald Reagan and Jack Eckerd, Clearwater, Florida, in 1974, when Jack Eckerd was running for United States Senator.

Below: Jack and Ruth Eckerd and President Gerald Ford at Jack Eckerd's swearing-in ceremony as general services administrator, 1975.

President Gerald Ford with Jack, Ruth, Nancy, and Richard Eckerd, 1977.

Jack Eckerd with President Jimmy Carter, 1977.

Left: Jack and Ruth Eckerd when he was running for governor, 1977.

Below: Jack Eckerd campaigning during 1978 gubernatorial race.

Jack Eckerd greeting a drugstore employee.
(UPI/Bettman Newsphotos.)

Right: Jack Eckerd and George Jenkins, founder and president of Publix Supermarkets, at the opening of a strip mall containing both an Eckerd drugstore and a Publix Supermarket.

Below: At the second annual meeting of PRIDE of Florida, Louie Wainwright, Warren E. Burger, Jack Eckerd, and Dr. Freddie L. Groomes were present.

Jack Eckerd and Chuck Colson. *(Photo used by permission Ellis Richman Photography © 1985.)*

Jack Eckerd with some of the boys at the Eckerd camp E-Toh-Kalu, 1986.

Jack and Ruth Eckerd at their North Carolina home, 1984.

Jack Eckerd playing Santa for one of his fourteen grandchildren.

The *Panacea*, crossing the Atlantic Ocean Gulf Stream, 1970.

12

In 1961, with twelve stores in operation, I made the decision to
"go public" by putting shares of Eckerd Drugs on the stock market.

The choice I made is considered by most entrepreneurs who build
fast-growing companies, and no single decision is ever more critical—or more permanent—than the decision to open a business to
public ownership. My reason was the most common one: I needed
more capital to sustain our rapid growth without constantly having
to borrow from the banks.

I had another reason for offering part of my ownership to the
public—my desire to see that our employees got part of the action.
I was eager to give them a stake in the growth and success of Eckerd
Drugs—not just a few top managers, but employees from the entire
spectrum of the company "family," and it was not feasible to take
that many people in as partners. The only alternative was to go
public, which would make it possible for them to be given stock as
bonuses or incentives or for them to buy it at preferred prices.

My need for cash was produced by the rapidly expanding opportunities we had for growth. The Publix connection was a part, but
only a part, of our developing reputation, and the principle that
success breeds success was now operating strongly in our favor. By
1960, I could see that our capacity to open and manage new stores
was virtually unlimited; we had a competent team in the corporate
office and stores, a proven formula for operating profitably, and

were becoming a "brand-name" company in the Tampa Bay area.

At that time, the bare-bones cost of opening a new store was about $150,000—about 20 percent of that going for fixtures and 80 percent to put inventory on the shelves and provide a small cash reserve of working capital. The Eckerd chain doubled its size every two years during the next sixteen years, a growth rate too fast for us to finance by using the stores' profits alone. To do so would have meant that every store must be profitable enough to duplicate itself every two years—an unreasonable expectation.

The company itself had strong profitability, well above 5 percent on volume, year after year, so we could have gone to the banks and borrowed the money for expansion, but I have an instinctive dislike of being permanently in debt. I just didn't like the idea of being in hock to bankers for the rest of my life. A new company that allows banks to finance its growth is often at their mercy during a recession, and that usually means decisions about the company's future will be made by bankers, who usually don't know as much about the retail business as the entrepreneur does.

By going public, I gave up private ownership of my company, but I maintained control of its destiny, and I cut my employees in on the action. I felt it was a good bargain.

In the original offering, which was handled by the Courts investment firm's Atlanta office, we sold 20 percent of the ownership of Eckerd's. The stock was offered at $10.00 a share, raising $2 million cash. It was a good case of having your cake and eating it, too: by keeping 80 percent of the ownership, I still controlled the company, but I now had the capital I needed to grow, without having to borrow. What the public was buying was a percentage of our earning potential, and since our profits were so strong, selling 200,000 shares at $10.00 a share was easy.

There are disadvantages in going public, of course, the first of which is that it costs more money to operate a public company. The sheer volume of paperwork required to comply with regulations, the need to communicate with stockholders and to process stock transfers, and the increased public accountability in all areas of the operation add to the company's cost of doing business.

A typical headache of operating a public company is keeping stockholders happy. In our case, at least in those red-hot years of the sixties and early seventies, we had no complaints from stockholders. We were doubling profits every two years, while simultaneously expanding volume at the same rate, a win-win situation virtually unheard of in a retail business. So our annual stockholders' meetings were lovefests. I would give the annual report of growth and earnings—"Well, we did it again!"—and we all celebrated another great year.

The biggest disadvantage of going public is the effect it has on the CEO and his use of time. As the years progressed, I spent more and more of my time with stock-market analysts and large stockholders, justifying why they should recommend our stock to their buyers or explaining why performance was not quite as good as the year before or projecting the future profit picture for the drugstore industry. I would have preferred to spend that time with my employees, in the drugstores, doing what I know and do best.

Nor is the executive's time the only problem—his decision-making strategy is also affected. The financial community is preoccupied with short-term success, with the profit picture this year or this quarter, and the tendency is that a CEO will respond by worrying too much about this year's performance, rather than what is best for the company five years or ten years down the road. As the owner of a private company, with no other owners to whom I must account, I had the luxury of making long-term decisions, even when they resulted in lower profits this year. As our percentage of public ownership increased, I increasingly felt the pressure of the annual report and the analysts' expectations.

We started as an over-the-counter stock, spent a few years on the American Stock Exchange, then finally, in 1968, went on the "big board" as a member of the New York Stock Exchange. That was an important benchmark for us and a special occasion for me personally. I am not normally much interested in symbols of success; my moments of satisfaction come in the work itself and not in the times of celebration, but I will admit that seeing the name *Jack Eckerd Corporation* go on the listing of the New York Stock Exchange was a significant experience for me. My corporate attorney, Norm Stallings, my president, Harry Roberts, and I went to New York with our wives; we stayed at the Plaza Hotel and went down to Wall Street the next day to be admitted officially to membership in the exchange.

But even then we decided not to have a big party, the usual corporate bash. I was still too tight to spend that much money, I suppose. The six of us had a quiet dinner at a restaurant in New York that night, then flew back home the next day and went to work.

I did allow myself one small goody to celebrate the occasion. I was walking down Fifth Avenue and, being an incurable retailer, was wandering in and out of department stores, just to see what they were selling and how they were displaying their merchandise. I went into Saks, and in the men's shoe department, a pair of alligator loafers caught my eye. They looked good, so I tried them on, and they were the most comfortable shoes I had ever worn.

"How much?" I asked the salesclerk.

"One hundred twenty-five dollars," she replied. I gulped. That was too much to pay for a pair of shoes in 1968, I thought, and was ready to thank her and head for the nearest exit. Then I remembered the report I had seen earlier that day, the breakdown of my net worth, and it suddenly struck me that if I could stroll onto the floor of the New York Stock Exchange as a new member, I could probably afford a pair of alligator shoes. I felt like saying, "Gimme *two* pairs!" So I bought the shoes—one pair only—and left Saks feeling like a profligate big spender.

There were other significant landmarks in the rise of our company to prominence. One was reaching the top of the list in *Fortune* magazine's ratings of overall corporate effectiveness among drugstore companies. This annual rating measures not just quantity, but quality; it told us we were not merely big, but we were good, that by all the various barometers of corporate success we were doing the best job for our stockholders. I remember looking at that list several times, just to make sure I wasn't seeing it wrong, and every time I looked, there we were in the number-one spot. That was a moment of special satisfaction.

Opening our hundredth store was also particularly satisfying, and opening our five-hundredth store may have been the most festive day of all. We announced a big chainwide sale to celebrate the occasion, and opened three new stores the same day—the four hundred ninety-eighth, four hundred ninety-ninth, and five hundredth stores. We had bought a company jet by that time—we were operating all over the southeastern United States—and we invited the current Miss America to join us and add to the excitement. We spent the day flying to each of those three stores, with Miss America in our entourage, and we had a big promotional party at each stop.

We still had young children at the time, and Ruth stayed home with them rather than going along for the fun. I came home late for dinner, buzzing excitedly about the day, telling her how beautiful Miss America was, and she gave me a single, withering look that told me she was having trouble sharing my euphoria at the moment. She had been home all day playing Mommy and pulling spaghetti out of the kids' hair while I had been cruising around in a jet with Miss America.

That summarizes, as well as any vignette I can recall, the "glamorous" life of the corporate executive's wife.

13

I am often asked by reporters or by students or young entrepreneurs to describe the ingredients of success in a new business venture.

My experience with Eckerd Drugs taught me that the company that has the best chance of rapid, solid growth is the company that:

1. Understands that its best asset is its employees.
2. Dares to do something different from what everyone else is doing.
3. Makes decisions on the basis of fairness to the public, the employees, and the stockholders.

In more recent years, I have realized that there is another ingredient of success that is often overlooked: asking God's help in making the right decisions. If I were managing a business today, that would go at the top of the list, but while I was building Eckerd Drugs, I still didn't understand that.

I realized that Eckerd's best asset was its employees; I think I intuitively understood that, from my earliest experiences in management. Many businesses lose sight of this, especially as they grow. It is easy for a CEO to spend so much time with a handful of top administrators that he considers their performance, rather than the performance of the wage earners in the stores, to be the critical difference in the success or failure of his company. The truth is that a retail business, large or small, lives or dies primarily on the basis of how effectively its front-line employees perform.

Much has been written, by those who have discussed my career in the business press, about my habit of personally visiting my drugstores and talking with the employees, even after we were a huge corporation. These visits have often been described as public-relations gestures, showing the flag for the corporation, to bolster the morale of our in-store personnel. The fact is that they were serious fact-finding trips; I believe strongly in the value of suggestions and feedback from employees at that level, and the best way to get it is to go into the stores and ask for it.

It is easy for corporate officials to underestimate how much little things mean to wage-earning employees and how frustrating it is for these employees to lodge complaints or make constructive suggestions in a way that they feel makes a difference and then have them not get through to the front office. I went into our stores not primarily to inspire workers, but to listen to them, and I always followed up on what I heard.

My pattern was to visit stores unannounced. As we grew larger and had several stores in a particular town I would pick a town and hit every store there, one after another. I made it a point to speak personally to every person working there. I had a computer printout prepared of the stores I would visit on a given day, and just before entering a store, I would review its performance the previous week, month, year, in the various merchandising areas—cosmetics, pharmacies, and the like. So when I walked in, I knew what was going on in the store at that particular time.

I never carried a clipboard or made notes while I was inside, and I rarely responded positively or negatively to complaints or suggestions I heard. I just listened and told the employees how much I appreciated their hard work and how much their honest input meant to me. As soon as I got back out to the car, I would make notes, scribbling down the things I had heard so I would be sure to follow up when I returned to the home office. Soliciting input and then not following up is worse than not going at all.

A lot of good ideas came from my visits to stores. No one knows more about what makes people buy lipstick than the cosmetician who sells it every day. No one knows more about the size and type of paper bag to use at the checkout than the cashier who fills them with products hundreds of times a day.

It was not unusual for me to walk into a drugstore at any time, day or night. It was good for morale. For years, it was a tradition for me to visit every store in the chain the week before Christmas; then we had to work hard just to make a "Christmas visit" to every store in the month of December; finally that tradition became completely impossible to maintain. But the visits to the stores, on a random basis, never stopped. I had to fight to avoid spending so much time with financial people and stock analysts, in meetings and seminars and public-relations events, that I had less contact with the people down in the stores. I tried to keep always in mind this one thing: almost every dollar we made, we made as a result of a retail transaction in an Eckerd drugstore. So it seemed only logical to me to stay in touch with the people who actually engaged in that retail transaction.

When I hit the trail, the Eckerd grapevine worked pretty well, and the word would travel that I was on the prowl in a given city. We had four stores in Tallahassee, when I visited there once in 1973. I went to the first store, made my usual contacts, and left. About ten minutes later, I drove up to the second Tallahassee store. All our stores had public address systems, and just as I walked through the front door, I heard the voice of the pharmacist boom out over the loudspeaker, "Okay, everybody, on your toes, the old man is on his way!"

A red-faced pharmacist greeted me that morning. Actually, I didn't mind at all; I knew they called me "the old man," and I knew we had a pretty good informal grapevine—I just didn't know it worked that fast!

I have been asked to assess the impact of my in-store visits on our success, but one simply cannot put a dollar value on that sort of thing. All I know is that it worked. It is the kind of thing that makes the difference between the great businesses and the others. It motivates employees, from the manager right down to the stockboy. And I don't think they are motivated by a feeling of fear, by the idea that they must be alert or else Mr. Eckerd might catch them doing something wrong.

I think the motivational power is subtler than that; it issues from the desire of every employee to be a person, to be accepted as an individual and not as a number or an invisible cog in a big machine. I don't know how many thousands of ideas I have had passed on to me in the stores, but I'm sure nine out of ten of them have been impractical. But the very idea that the employee would pass it on and *can* pass it on is worth something. It's something they talk about, at home that night with the family; it makes the job more meaningful. Also, there *is* that tenth idea, the one that does turn out to have practical, bottom-line value, that makes sifting through the others worthwhile. Do you know who was motivated most by those visits? Jack Eckerd!

The big winner in any competitive industry will not be the company that merely manages well, but the one that breaks out of the pack, first, with a new idea. That requires risk taking, and in business, as in the rest of life, the long shots yield the big payoffs.

In my opinion, three innovations in our early history are examples of breaking new ground, and were inarguably critical to our gaining a leadership position in the industry. The first of these was the successful challenge to the so-called Fair Trade Law, which made possible our whole self-service approach to retailing, with the ensuing publicity that brought us to public attention for the first time.

Our second major innovation was senior-citizen discounts. In 1987, the concept of discount prices for older consumers is so commonplace that one must be reminded there was a time when it was unknown, an untried idea. We first introduced it to our customers in 1956, and it became one of the keys to our early success.

Our motives, when we first came up with the idea, were not altogether altruistic; I would enjoy taking credit for being so noble, but the truth is that I realized it would assist us in selling more products. Senior-citizen discounts were helpful to a lot of older people, who were living on fixed incomes. However, it was also helpful to Eckerd's. This was a win-win situation, and I liked that kind of deal.

In the beginning, we gave the discount—originally 20 percent off—only to persons aged sixty-five or older, at least half of whose income came from Social Security or retirement policies, and the discount itself was restricted to prescriptions, over-the-counter drugs, and sickroom supplies. Obviously, the cost of monitoring that very narrow set of qualifications would have been prohibitive, so we started with an "honor system."

The idea was a tremendous success, far beyond our expectations. By older consumers, who are more likely to be price conscious and who spend a larger proportion of their income on drugs and medicines, the discount was considered substantial, and we found ourselves rapidly becoming identified by that segment of the market as the drugstore that cared about senior citizens.

In the demographic mix of central Florida, that image in the market gave us a tremendous boost. Obviously, other retailers soon copied our program; we expanded the types of products on which the discount was offered, and that, too, was matched. But however many of our competitors joined the parade, we were there first, and that gave us a permanent edge.

Senior-citizen discounts would eventually become a standard feature of marketing in such diverse industries as the airlines, hotels, banking, restaurants, and almost any product or service imaginable. In the 1980s, the percentage of American consumers over the age of sixty-five is so large and growing larger so rapidly that every college kid in Economics 101 realizes the need for marketing strategies aimed at that segment of the population. Thirty years ago, however, that was not the case. Our senior-citizen discount program was an example of trying something different; we were ahead of our time, and it paid off handsomely for us.

Another breakthrough, which had a similarly powerful impact on us, was the idea of offering two-for-one film. Drugstores do big business with photo processing and the sale of film and photo supplies. Someone in a staff meeting in the mid-fifties came up with the idea of offering customers an extra copy of every print they had developed at an Eckerd drugstore. "One to keep—one to give away." It was an idea with obvious appeal; the question was whether or not it was economically feasible.

At that time, our film developing was being done on a contract basis by an independent processor. We talked him into giving us the extra print at no additional cost, on the premise that he would make up the difference in additional volume. He agreed to take that risk, primarily because he wanted to keep our account and keep his equipment busy. With that deal made, we had our own profit margins preserved, so we launched a promotional campaign offering two-for-one photo developing.

It was the hottest thing that ever hit the photo-developing business. Our volume soared; the attractiveness of getting that extra print at no extra cost was far greater than we had hoped, and it made an immediate, enormous difference in our business. It was one of those deals in which everybody won: the customer, because he got two prints; the drugstore, because we got a bigger share of the photo business; and the film developer, who came out ahead because, even though his profit margin was only half as much, his volume was three times bigger, so he made more money.

Our photo business got so much bigger that eventually we built our own processing company, and still today Eckerd Drugs is the largest single customer of Eastman Kodak photo paper. Once again, our competitors were playing catch-up; they soon were forced to match our deal, and the two-for-one offer is standard in the marketplace today. But being there first paid off for us, and our company is still regarded today as the leader in film processing.

In all three of these critical policy decisions—the "Fair Trade" suit, senior-citizen discounts, and two-for-one film—the fundamental rule of fairness was faithfully observed. In each case, everyone came out ahead, except our competitors. The consumer clearly profited from our aggressiveness, because each innovation resulted in lower prices at the checkout counter. The stockholders profited, because the increased volume we generated made our corporate bottom line juicier than ever. The employees profited, because their jobs were made more secure by virtue of working for a profitable and growing company. Not one of these three major initiatives occurred at the expense of the employees; we were not making higher profits by squeezing more work from our staff; we were making higher profits by intelligent marketing policy. When a company maximizes profits in that way, everyone wins.

14

Rex Farrior

What was it about Jack that made him so successful? The man knew how to make a decision, and it was usually a good decision. Not always—I thought he made a big mistake once or twice, but I never told him about it.

At one time he had decided to go into the liquor-store business, and I thought that was a mistake, but he was going to do it anyway, so I didn't say anything. Then he decided it wasn't the thing he wanted to do after all.

That was in the very beginning, when he wasn't making any money to speak of. Just had a handful of little stores. He told me, "I believe I'll get into the cut-price liquor business." Under the Tampa law at that time, there were all the liquor stores in town they intended to allow, so to open a new one, you had to buy a license from an existing store, then have it transferred to your name by proceeding through the city council. It was a routine thing, but that's what you had to do.

Jack asked me to find him a liquor license, so I rode around to the bars at night until I found a place over in West Tampa. I could tell the fella was in bad financial condition, because he didn't have over

$50 or $60 worth of stock on his shelves. So I arranged to buy his license and stock for a total of $500.

I applied to the city council for the license to be transferred to Jack, so he could open up a liquor store next to one of his drugstores. Under the city ordinance, the application had to pass three readings. It went through the first two readings with no trouble. But just before the third reading, a city councillor went to see Jack and said it would take $1,000 to get it through the third reading. It was a bribe, pure and simple, and I told Jack that was just the way business was done in those days. It was not too uncommon, and everyone understood that's just the way it was.

But Jack would have none of it. He told me, "Forget it. Just forget it. If I can't do business on top of the table, I don't do business at all!" He meant it. I asked if he wanted me to find him another license, and he said, "No, just forget the whole idea of getting into the liquor business." After that, he would have none of it. So that's why he never got into the liquor business.

By the way, in dealing with that fella we bought the license from, I had stipulated that if for some reason the transfer didn't pass the city council, we wouldn't pay the $500. Good thing, too. We got out of that one and never had to pay the $500.

Another thing about Jack: he always made sure everybody who worked for him had a piece of the action—that way they weren't just working for Jack, they were working for themselves. At one point, he put most of his stock in the Eckerd Corporation into a trust—one of my law partners drew up the trust, not me—and it permitted employees to buy Eckerd stock considerably below the market price. That stock grew, many times over. He made millionaires out of many of his key employees and managers.

Some people felt that Eckerd almost worked himself to death in those days, but I never worried about him much. His employees loved him. When he ran for office, lots of them, whom he never even knew about, went out and worked for him. I think it's safe to call him a financial wizard, and I've known a few businessmen in my time.

One day I got a call from a friend of mine who was president of Florida Christian College. He was hunting money, so of course he wanted Jack and me to have lunch with him. I said, "Jim, getting three busy men together for lunch is almost impossible. Just send me some literature, and I'll see that Jack gets it." So he did. I went over to have dinner with Jack one night and gave him that stuff. He looked at it, but he didn't say a word. I know Jack—you don't sell Jack, except by the merchandise you have. If he doesn't buy your merchandise, you can forget it.

About a month later, I got a beautiful letter from the college president, thanking me, because Jack had sent him 1,000 shares of stock. After that, the stock doubled two for one five times, and three for two once. The price per share went straight up, too. I figure that little block of stock was eventually worth a very substantial amount of money.

I've said many times—when a man has money, if you want to judge him, find out two things: how he made it and what he does with it, and by those standards, Jack's 100 percent.

15

For me, the 1960s were consumed by the drive to build the Eckerd Corporation into a major force in the retail drug industry, and by almost any standard of measurement, that was achieved.

The 1970s were a period in which I entered another field—that of politics and public service. That arena provided the same excitement and challenges of the business world, though perhaps with more frustration and, in a certain sense, fewer tangible rewards.

Soon after the decade began, I decided to run for governor.

The decision came abruptly and without warning to almost everyone, including myself. I had no previous political involvement, other than voting like any other good citizen. I was not part of the "club" in the Republican party in the state of Florida. I had no network of political friends or supporters and no long-term strategy for the future.

So why did I run for governor?

Very simple: I was appalled by the behavior of the governor we had, and it appeared that no one else in the Republican party was going to oppose him for reelection. So I decided to do it myself.

The governor, in 1970, was Claude Kirk, the first Republican to serve in that position in Florida in 100 years. I had been a Republican all my life and, like many Florida Republicans, was delighted that our party finally occupied the governor's mansion. But our pleasure soon dissipated into disappointment and embarrassment as

Kirk fumbled his way through his four-year term. I was offended by his public behavior and chagrined that he was a Republican. It seemed to me that a lot of people felt as I did, but as the 1970 election year neared, no credible Republican was willing to challenge an incumbent governor within the party.

I could not stand seeing Kirk get a free ride to the general election, so I threw my hat into the ring.

There were deeper personal reasons for my decision, I'm sure. Nothing is as simple as it seems. By this time, I had made a lot of money in the drugstore business, mostly in the state of Florida, and I felt a great sense of gratitude for that. The state had been good to me and my family. I began to ask myself what I had ever done as a way of repaying this debt. A friend said to me once, when I was griping about how things were being run in Tallahassee, "You businessmen like to talk about how terrible government is, but what have you ever done about it?" Making this race was partially a way of paying back the system for all it had given me. It was my way of getting involved. It may have been misguided—I'm sure Claude Kirk thought so—but I was sincerely doing what I thought was good for the state. I still feel that way.

Also, to tell the truth, I was temporarily getting a bit bored by the drugstore business. I had been holding onto the bull's tail of this business, practically to the exclusion of everything else, for almost twenty years. The job of running an ever-expanding drugstore chain, year after year, was becoming less exciting. I guess I was looking for a new challenge, so I said to myself, "Why not?"

Though I did not understand it at the time, the restlessness I felt in 1969 was one of the first symptoms of a serious problem: I had a peculiar kind of hunger inside me that all my success in business had not satisfied. There was something missing in my life, and I was beginning to sense it, vaguely at first, then more and more strongly, until finally it set the stage for the most critical decision of my life. But that was later. For now I knew only that I had heard the siren song of politics.

The idea of running began to form in my mind in the last few months of 1969. I did not consult very many people about the decision, because down deep I knew what I wanted to do, and I didn't want anyone to talk me out of it. I did ask Ruth, of course, and she encouraged me to do it. "Well, it's going to involve the family, too, you know," I told her. "I know," she replied, "and I don't particularly like that part of it, but we'll support you. Just don't expect me to get up in front of people and make speeches."

They did support me, every member of the family, right down to the dog. Everyone was involved, and I don't think I'm wrong in thinking everyone enjoyed it. Ours was not a conventional political campaign. It was more of an amateur's crusade; we had so much energy and idealism and so little hard-nosed political savvy that when I recall the way we tore around the state in that campaign, even I get amused.

The amazing thing about it was that we ran a very strong race, forced the incumbent governor into a primary runoff, and paved the way for his resounding defeat in the general election. We barely knew what we were doing, but apparently the voters responded.

I announced my candidacy in January of 1970. I took a leave from the corporation and took myself off the Eckerd Drugs payroll. At my first press conference, the reporters asked the predictable question: "What political campaigns have you been in before?"

"None," I said.

"We know you have been inactive in Florida," they replied, "but what about earlier in life—you must have run for something up in Wilmington or Erie?"

"Nothing," I repeated.

"Not even dogcatcher?" they insisted, a bit incredulously.

"Not even dogcatcher," I affirmed.

Then one of them asked the question I would hear a hundred times: "If you've never run for anything at all before, why in the world are you running for governor?"

I responded to him as I would a hundred times more: "Well, you gotta start someplace."

That was a facetious reply, and it always got a laugh from reporters, but it was the truth. I had the same feeling that most people have—that the government was an inefficient bureaucracy not attuned to the needs and desires of the people and that I could make a change. I had to start someplace.

It was an exciting year. The race started with both Ruth and me breaking our legs and stumping around the state in look-alike plaster casts. I went skiing up in the Laurentian Mountains, in Canada, a week before announcing my candidacy, and broke a bone in my left leg. The week after the announcement, Ruth and I were on a friend's boat in Tampa Bay, watching the start of a sailboat race. Ruth stepped backward on the deck of that boat, right into an open hatch, and broke a bone in her right ankle. So we started the campaign with matching broken legs, hers on the right, mine on the left, and a photograph went out over the news wire that showed us sitting together on stage at a political rally, each with a plaster cast.

Once the race began and the media and Governor Kirk saw I was a serious candidate, we were caught up in a whirlwind. I bought an old DC-3, painted FLORIDA NEEDS JACK ECKERD along the fuselage, talked a retired air force colonel named Paul Ponder into serving as pilot, and barnstormed the state. For short trips, we used a motor home and the family station wagon.

As the campaign developed, the single biggest negative issue used against me was my wealth. I never fully understood why voters are so often unwilling to support a wealthy candidate, but that usually seems to be the case. In the press, I was invariably described as a "drugstore tycoon," a "multimillionaire," the "wealthy head of a drugstore empire," or in some other fashion that called attention to my financial status. The focus was invariably on my wealth, and that hurt me with the voters.

The public somehow has great suspicion of a wealthy man who runs for office. Many people believe that anyone who has hit the jackpot economically, as I had, must be dishonest. Rich people may have been smart enough to cover it up, the public suspects, but somewhere along the way they must have ripped people off, because there is no way to accumulate that kind of wealth honestly.

Changing that public attitude was virtually impossible, unless you are a Kennedy or a Rockefeller. In my speeches and advertising, I tried to emphasize the obvious point that a rich man is not likely to steal from the public once he gets into office. Maybe that helped a little, but I never really outran the wealth issue.

If a challenge was what I needed, I found plenty in the uphill fight I faced. I must admit that I got turned on by the whole thing. My adrenaline started to flow, and I put in ungodly hours every day and enjoyed it. I even got to where I enjoyed making speeches, although that was never my strong suit. I hated the days when the organizers of a rally would promise 500 people, and I would fly halfway across the state, and only 50 showed up. That was tough to take.

As we neared election day, the Kirk campaign began to run scared, or at least that's the way it seemed to us. There was a third candidate in the race, a man named Skip Bafalis, and though I knew I had little chance of beating Kirk outright, I felt a growing hope that he would fail to gain a majority in the three-man race and would be forced to face me alone in a runoff.

In the end, that is exactly what happened. When the polls closed and the votes were counted on September 8, Kirk had 165,000 votes (47 percent), to my 133,000, with Bafalis getting 48,000. We were jubilant. We felt that for an incumbent governor to be forced into a runoff in the primary of his own party was an eloquent statement that he was not an effective leader of his party or the people of Florida. In that sense, we had made our point and could be happy about it.

Politics doesn't work that way, however; once a little success is injected into the bloodstream, the fever is hard to cure. Rather than relaxing with the knowledge that we had made our case with the voters, we entered the three weeks before the runoff with fresh energy and dreams of winning it all.

In the runoff race, I was blind-sided by a bit of campaign chicanery that cost me dearly. I was running dead even in the polls until about a week before the runoff. Kirk and I met in a debate in Jacksonville, which was televised all around the state. My staff was nervous about the debate. "You've got to be alert," they cautioned me. "This guy is running scared, and he's liable to do a number on you." And he did.

We reached the end of the debate, and each of us had time for a final summation. When his turn came, Kirk reached under his podium and pulled out a paperback book. It was a book about marijuana. He showed it to the crowd, describing it as a book that promoted the use of illegal drugs, and told the TV audience that he had bought it that day in an Eckerd drugstore. "This guy is telling you he can run the state of Florida, and this is the kind of stuff he sells in his stores." He waved the book at the cameras. "I don't think he deserves a chance to run the state of Florida, when he can't even keep books like this out of his drugstores."

I was flabbergasted. He ranted on in that vein until his time ended, and a moment later the "debate" was over and we were off the air without my having a chance to even say how ridiculous the whole thing was.

That one cheap trick summed up the whole Kirk campaign. I'll say one thing—the governor was quite a showman, and the press loved it. I tried to recoup, but it was too near election day to do so. Ironically, one of my staff members went out and found the same book—a completely harmless one, by the way—in the University of South Florida campus bookstore, which Claude Kirk indirectly controlled. We announced that to the press, but our "rebuttal" got buried in the back pages of the papers. Obviously, the whole issue was sheer distortion and demagoguery, and he knew it. But that, unfortunately, is politics, and I went to the polls on September 29 a sadder but wiser candidate.

Kirk beat me in the runoff, then went on to lose resoundingly in the general election to Reuben Askew, a Democrat who turned out to be a very popular governor. When it was over, I had no regrets about my decision to run. I learned a lot in that campaign; it was sort of a crash course on the affairs of the state of Florida, from top to bottom, and I was a better man when it was over.

There was only one thing about it I hated: losing. It ate my guts out at the time. Time heals all wounds, and now I chuckle about it, but at the time it hurt. The pain of losing was not like that of losing in a business deal; I knew how to handle that. Losing at politics was a more personal kind of rejection. I would have lots of practice at it before I was through, but I never learned how to lose without hurting.

16

Charles Paul Conn

What is the best way to get a true picture of a past political campaign?

Probably not from candidates themselves. Personal political memories are notoriously faulty, distorted by the intense emotions of the race itself and by the fact that the candidate's perspective is so limited. For veteran campaigners, there is another problem: the races tend to run together in one's memory; as the years go by, the moods of one campaign are often included in the recounting of another.

The most accurate picture of a bygone political contest probably comes from the newspaper files of that year. It is a rare politician who does not view the media with a certain amount of paranoia; in a three-way race, all three candidates suspect the press is out to get them. The office seeker himself rarely trusts the journalistic record to provide an objective history of a campaign.

In the combined record of two or three dozen papers, however, over the course of a long campaign, the true picture of a race is faithfully captured. In the welter of news stories, editorials, and interviews lies the reality of a campaign as the public perceived it—

the ups and downs, the pace and flavor, free of the distortions that will occur in the candidate's memory in years to come.

The microfilm files from that 1970 campaign show that Eckerd was viewed at first as a Don Quixote, a well-meaning novice engaged in a futile fight against an entrenched incumbent. As the race went on, however, he became recognized as a political force of considerable strength, and editorialists began to urge Floridians to vote for him.

Feature articles from early 1970 portrayed him from the same few angles: his family, his open and informal style, his personal honesty, and without exception, his wealth. Stories speculated on the exact size of his fortune; one feature analyzed the value of Eckerd Corporation stock (it was on the New York Stock Exchange), questioned whether it would rise or fall if he won, and noted that he personally owned 2.5 million shares at twenty-eight dollars a share. (The stock ticked *up* by half a point the day after election. Evidently his stockholders wanted him to stay in the company.)

Other writers found positive things to say about the prospect of a rich man in the governor's mansion. One paper, analyzing Eckerd's income-tax returns, pointed out that in the five years prior to the race, he had averaged an annual income of $717,000, of which he had contributed an average $420,000 annually to various charities. How can a man be faulted for making so much money, the writer argued, when he gives most of it away?

Another reporter found a fresh angle by describing the down-to-earth style of a man who was most often characterized as the "tycoon" of a business empire. The writer offered this picture: "Some politicians ride jets, or limousines with bodyguards. Millionaire Jack Eckerd showed up at the Sunshine Speedway Bar-B-Q Tuesday night in shirt sleeves, driving his own slightly muddy Ford station wagon and accompanied only by his wife and passle of their many kids."

The Eckerd campaign obviously tried to find a positive slant on the wealth issue. A campaign ad that appeared frequently in the state's newspapers reads: "One nice thing about electing a rich man governor—no one can buy him. Jack Eckerd, the man with no strings attached.''

In all this talk of money, there was never, in any paper in the state, a hint of financial impropriety on Eckerd's part. To the contrary, he is portrayed as being unusually meticulous in the conduct of his personal financial affairs. One journalist reported: ''He's so honest he even listed eleven dollars for party cookies as part of his campaign expenses.''

As a political rookie, Eckerd had difficulty raising money for his campaign, a problem compounded by the public discussion of his wealth. A statewide wire-service story in July said the candidate had put $800,000 of his own money into the campaign treasury. An interview with the Miami *Herald* is typical of the way he handled the issue:

QUESTION: ''Why are you spending so much money on the campaign?''

ANSWER: ''The biggest problem I've had is getting contributions. I wish you'd stop printing about my wealth. People don't realize that all my money is in toothpaste and drugs, and I'm out madly borrowing from every bank in Florida to forward my candidacy. It's expensive. I'm the only citizen candidate. All the others are holders of high elective office.''

The Eckerd staff tried also to defuse this issue by attacking it head-on, with another set of full-page newspaper ads, which read: ''Some people say that Jack Eckerd is wrong to spend so much money. Others disagree . . . ,'' followed by a list of some two hundred charitable agencies to which he had given money. Total value of the contributions: ''$5,140,821.64.''

It was an impressive ad, but the unrelenting discussion of Eckerd's personal fortune seemed at times to obscure the other, more substantial issues he tried to raise. In the end, the typical voter, who went to the polls with only fragmentary information and images gained from the campaign media coverage, undoubtedly thought of Eckerd as a rich man who ran for lack of something better to do. One newspaper called him ''a millionaire who chose to run for

governor rather than find a new business interest or spend more time
on his sailboat.''

Eckerd's recollection is that the state's newspapers were rather
evenly divided in editorial support of him and Kirk, but the record
shows a far more decisive support of the challenger than that. Ultimately, a big majority (one count shows twenty-one to four) of the
state's newspapers came down on his side. Some of their endorse-
ments summarize the positive opinions they developed during the
campaign:

Naples *Daily News*: ''We submit that state government can benefit from a business-like administration which Eckerd can deliver.''

Miami *News*: ''We were impressed by his high level of intelligence, forthright manner, clear grasp of sensitive state issues, and
proven record as an executive.''

Fort Lauderdale *News*: ''He combines a philosophy and qualities
that make him an outstanding nominee. His motivations are of the
highest order. Eckerd blends incisiveness with an idealistic enthusiasm which does not cloud his vision to the realities of a situation.
He would come to the office wholly untainted by political commit-
ments.''

St. Petersburg *Times*: ''In the campaign he has been a David vs.
Goliath, turning the astonishing feat of drawing the incumbent governor into a runoff. He has a remarkable ability to organize and
manage. He has the skill, directness, and ethics which merit his
party's nomination.''

Other major papers around the state, including such prominent
dailies as the Miami *Herald* and the Tampa *Tribune*, endorsed his
candidacy, all the more remarkable when one considers that they
were favoring a political greenhorn over an incumbent governor.

Editorial writers, of course, cast only one vote each on election
day, just as any other citizen does, and in the end, the Eckerd
enthusiasm and crusading spirit were not enough to beat Kirk at the
polls.

Eckerd cast his vote, then awaited the verdict, surrounded by his
campaign workers, at a motel ballroom in Fort Lauderdale. The

results were clear early in the evening, and Eckerd, rather than holding out for a midnight miracle, conceded to Kirk at 8:35 P.M.

A Fort Lauderdale reporter, describing the loser's election-night headquarters scene, showed that Eckerd could still match the tears of his supporters with his own sense of humor. "For more than an hour," the reporter says, "Jack Eckerd, Republican loser, walked around the Las Olas ballroom at the Holiday Inn, blaming no one but himself. He was fifty-seven years old. Asked how he felt, the candidate replied, 'This is better than the morgue; there they make you stretch out.' "

The Miami *Herald* quoted him, that same night, as summing up the race this way: "It was worth every cent. If I hadn't of run, ten years from now I would have said to myself, 'Chicken!' "

17

I would run twice more and lose twice more, before my days as a candidate ended, but I had no prospects of that in the fall of 1970, and immediately resumed my role as chief executive officer of the Eckerd Corporation.

I am rather reluctant to admit it, but running the corporation was never as interesting to me after that race as it had been before my exposure to politics. When I went back to the corporation, it seemed a bit dull. As much as I had always enjoyed the challenge of building a business, I confess now that to some degree I had lost my drive and enthusiasm for the corporate battles.

One of the problems was with the business itself: it had gotten so big, it was too impersonal to be as rewarding as before. In some ways, running the Eckerd drugstore operation was never as much fun after the first fifty to one hundred stores. Of necessity, the job became more complex and less personal; that is a typical problem with rapid growth. I was never as comfortable being a corporate executive as being an entrepreneur, and I understood that fact better when I returned to my office after the 1970 election.

By 1972, the corporation had 7,000 employees, was operating 342 drugstores, owned a small chain of department stores called J. Byrons's Department Stores, and had acquired two unrelated subsidiaries: Gray Security Services and Kurman Company, a major food service firm with operations in Florida and Latin America. The

CEO of that kind of corporation has less time for the daily contact with front-line employees which I enjoyed so much and which politics offered so abundantly.

Before long I began to eye the 1974 election with a certain personal interest.

The prize this time was not the governor's mansion, but the United States Senate seat, which had been held by Edward Gurney, a fellow Republican. Going into that election year, no one anticipated a primary race; Gurney had done a good job in Washington and was seeking reelection.

In the early summer, however, the seat was suddenly thrown up for grabs when Gurney was accused of collecting $233,000 from building contractors in return for preferred treatment in the granting of federal government contracts. I had a great deal of sympathy for Gurney and would not have run against him; but in mid-July he was indicted on charges of bribery, conspiracy, and perjury and withdrew as a candidate for reelection.

Suddenly the Republican nomination was available to whoever could seize it. The first major figure to enter the race was Paula Hawkins, a popular public service commissioner; others were expected to announce at any time, and my phone began to ring incessantly, with leading Republicans from around the state urging me to run.

It was, I confess, exactly what I wanted to hear. Since 1970, I had reflected on what I would do differently if I ever ran again. I figured the experience I had gained would make me a more effective campaigner, and certainly the exposure had increased my name-identity statewide. I was itching to get into another political fight, and this was shaping up as a good one. I don't think I required much persuasion to say yes.

In the 1974 race, my campaign was a little slicker, better organized, with more of the strategy and decisions being directed by political professionals. In 1970, I had underestimated the degree of specialization involved in a campaign; I was so naive, I was shocked to learn that one's television image is more important than his platform. In this race, I used TV much more effectively than before.

Because of the timing of Gurney's withdrawal, the primary race was fast and furious. When I announced my intention to run, the other possible candidates decided to avoid the race, leaving Paula Hawkins and me to fight it out. I won the primary decisively, by almost a two-to-one vote, and faced the Democratic candidate, Richard Stone of Miami, in the general election.

In the campaign itself, I had one old problem and two new ones. The old problem was money. This time, the rules were different; a new federal law had been passed since 1970, which limited to $35,000 the amount of money a candidate could contribute to his own campaign. (The law was repealed soon afterward.) As a result the amount of money I personally spent on my campaign was not an issue, but the "rich man" label still was.

There was a frustrating irony at work: we had great difficulty raising money for the campaign, because of the perception of me as a wealthy individual who could afford to take care of his own expenses. Our fund raisers were frequently met with, "Eckerd's loaded; he doesn't need *my* money!" So my wealth made it hard to raise money, but the law kept us from using my own. As a result, Stone beat me badly in fund raising, $800,000 to my $400,000 (which is peanuts today). We had to cancel most of our television spots in the last two weeks of the campaign, because our treasury was depleted. The "rich" candidate couldn't campaign because he had no money.

I had two new problems: Watergate and John Grady.

Watergate exploded as a national scandal, in 1974, and was the issue that dominated our Senate race. I was constantly, every day, several times a day, asked about Watergate. I tried to explain to the press that I knew nothing about Watergate. "I wasn't there that night," I told them. "I don't know as much about it as you do."

Still, the questions came. I had trouble getting people to talk about the issues between Stone and me, because of the obsessive interest in Richard Nixon and coverups and scandal in high places. Watergate was the cross every Republican candidate had to bear in

1974, all across the nation. There was nothing to do but answer questions as intelligently as possible and hope the public interest in it would subside.

My third problem was a third-party candidate, John Grady, who ran an extremely effective campaign. Grady, a physician from northern Florida, ran under the banner of the American Party. He was an ultraconservative; next to him, I looked like a flaming liberal. He was a great campaigner, and he worried me; I knew that most of the votes he received would come from my potential supporters rather than Stone's.

My staff told me not to worry about Grady. "Just ignore him," they said, expressing the conventional political wisdom about third-party candidates. "You've got 87 percent name recognition; he's got only 2 percent. If you campaign against him, you'll just give him more exposure, so ignore him." They assured me he would get 5 percent of the vote, no more, no less, and we could win without that 5 percent.

I had an uneasy feeling about Grady, right up until election day. I would go into little towns for an outdoor rally, and there would be more Grady signs in the crowd than Eckerd signs. It seemed to me that he was making more headway with the voters than we had expected.

But we decided to ignore John Grady. Well, we ignored him, and we were wrong. When the ballots were counted, he got 15 percent of the vote, not 5 percent, and that made the difference in the race.

The ordeal of waiting for the results on election night was much longer and more traumatic than it had been in 1970. This one was a cliff-hanger. The polls rated the race as a toss-up all the way, which was exactly how it turned out. I lost by less than 2 percent of the vote. It wasn't until the wee hours of the morning that we knew the verdict. Florida's Senate seat was the very last race "called" by the national television networks that morning, and the fact that it was so close only made it harder to accept the loss.

The pain of losing was reduced by the presence of a few close friends, especially George Mariani, who was always there, in good times and bad. George is a neighbor whose friendship goes back to my early sailing days. He raised money for me in every campaign, was there to celebrate a few victories, but more important, to suffer with me through the defeats. I couldn't ask for a better friend than him, and I never needed one more than I did after that 1974 loss at the polls.

My final shot at elective office came in 1978, when I ran again for governor and lost again in a close race, this time to Bob Graham, who went on to become a very popular Democratic governor.

By now, I had paid my dues in the Republican party and was sought by the party leaders as a candidate. This time it actually did require a lot of persuasion; I had no great desire to run again, having taken my lumps twice already, but my friends in the party convinced me that it would serve the public good for me to run and that I had a great chance of winning.

Before declaring my candidacy, my staff authorized a statewide poll to determine, among other things, what fellow Republican would best enhance the ticket as my running mate. (In Florida, the governor and lieutenant governor run as a team on a single ticket.) In the polls, one individual far exceeded all others: my old adversary in the 1974 primary, Paula Hawkins.

The professionals on my staff practically salivated at the prospect of Paula and me running together; they thought her image as the champion of the consumer, developed as a public service commissioner, would make us a "dream ticket." I was not sure whether Paula and I could get along well enough to run together but was eager to create a winning combination, so I asked her to join the ticket, and she accepted.

We started the race well ahead of Graham in all the polls, but he was a good campaigner, and gradually our lead eroded. It was a clean race, contested on the typical bread-and-butter issues that usually divide Republicans and Democrats, and both sides kept our campaigns at a high ethical level throughout the autumn.

The worst flap of the race came not from the Democratic camp, but from within our own ranks, triggered by a moment of indiscretion on my part. I was on a crowded elevator in Miami one day during the campaign, when someone remarked about how strongheaded Paula was and how she might be difficult to work with if we were elected. "Listen," I retorted. "There's only going to be one governor up there in Tallahassee, not two, and Paula will have to get used to that."

I should have known better. A reporter who was on the elevator noted the comment and wrote a major story around it, which went out all over the state. A horrendous uproar ensued. Paula, who was campaigning in a different part of the state, read the quote and got indignant at what she felt was a slight to her importance as a member of the team. She responded with a few choice comments of her own. Before we realized it, the two of us were engaged in a public exchange via the media, which was puffed into a full-scale intramural fight. The Graham people must have loved it; when we should have been aiming all our guns at him, we were taking potshots at each other, or so it seemed.

That little spat blew over, but Paula and I were never a really good team, and I think the public sensed that. It was a marriage of political convenience, for both of us, and it did not work as well as we hoped it would.

Ultimately, none of that mattered very much. The bottom line was the same as in 1974: I was beaten in November in a close race. There were no hard feelings in that race between Graham and me; we both ran hard and well, and I lost. That is how the process works.

There was one additional result of that 1978 election: it finally cured me of ballot-box fever. I have never been tempted to run again since then. I finally learned that, like it or not, the people of Florida were not willing to accept me in a statewide election.

I have no regrets at all about running. The part of it I liked least was losing, but even with that, I don't regret running. People who allow the chance of failure to stop them are going to miss a lot in life. Anything worthwhile requires the risk of losing, and that is a risk I have always been willing to take.

Ruth Eckerd

When Jack decided to run for governor that first time, I was probably as responsible for talking him into it as anyone. We had a Republican governor who was an embarrassment to the party, and I needled Jack to do something about it. I knew Jack to be a special person, so I felt everybody else in the state would jump in and feel the same way.

I was too much the idealist. We both were. We were like children playing in politics, that first time. We were so naive—I think back and marvel. After that first campaign we all realized we had done some pretty dumb things, and we thought we would never be in another one. I don't really remember how we changed our minds about running again, but we did.

The worst thing about all those campaigns, to me, was making speeches. I hated to make speeches and refused to do so at first, but gradually I was drawn into it. During the last campaign, I had a slide show, and that made it easier. We all did our part. The days I hated most were when I would get up at six o'clock in the morning and fly across the state in a little airplane, sometimes in thunderstorms, to make a speech. I've never been brave about flying, but in a campaign, you fly in terrible weather, because you have to get there, to the coffee or luncheon or whatever, because other people have worked to arrange it, and you can't let them down.

As far as I was concerned, all three campaigns were tough. The newspaper coverage was the worst part of it; it would just eat at me, the things that were said about Jack. The criticism bothered me a lot more than it did him. He would just toss it off and tell me not to pay any attention to it.

I would read things in the papers I knew were not true, and I would just fume. I don't think most people in the press ever realized how honest Jack's motives were for running. When editorials criticized him, I would seethe for days; I took it all too personally, I suppose, but I got mad and hurt.

I can look back and be glad we didn't win, but at the time, it was devastating. It was always devastating to lose, even in the first one, when we didn't have much chance to win. You gear your life toward that campaign, all the excitement, the highs and lows, good news and bad news, then all of a sudden it's all over, all that work down the tubes, and it's hard to take.

There were good things that came out of those races, of course. The best part is that we now have friends all over Florida, people who helped us and worked for us, whom we will never forget. Even though the campaign could be pretty grueling, it was also fun and exciting. It taught us a lot, and most of all it helped me appreciate more the life I had with Jack, the little things, just having him around.

After every race was over, I appreciated more than ever the simple pleasures we had, the chance to relax, to play tennis together, to spend a little time at home with our family.

18

Elective office is the glamorous side of the political process, but there is another side, just as important, to which I was introduced after my campaign defeat in 1974.

While I was still considering my future options following the narrow defeat, I received a call from someone in President Gerald Ford's office at the White House. I took the call, thinking it was probably a routine courtesy call from Ford, whom I had come to know on a casual basis.

Instead, the caller said President Ford wanted me to consider becoming the United States ambassador to Trinidad and Tobago.

The offer was totally unexpected. Ford and I were not exactly old buddies, and I had always thought of ambassadorships to small countries as plums reserved for the president's friends. Besides, I wasn't even sure I knew where Trinidad and Tobago were!

That night, I told Ruth about the call and laughed about it, but she did not dismiss it so lightly. She asked me one of my favorite questions: "Why not?" As we discussed it, the idea of accepting the assignment sounded not so unreasonable after all. My best option, other than that, was to return to the leadership of the corporation, and that didn't sound very challenging. When I entered the Senate race, I had resigned as CEO of the company, rather than merely taking a leave of absence as I had in 1970. The new president,

Stewart Turley, was doing a good job, and I felt the company no longer needed me on a day-to-day basis. I was still chairman of the board and chaired its executive committee, but I was no longer running the operation. If I ever intended to commit myself to full-time public service, this seemed a good time to do it.

Ruth and I inspected the Trinidad offer from every angle that night and finally decided we should pursue it further. "It might be a lot of fun," Ruth said, "so why don't you check into it further?"

I called back to Washington and told Ford's personnel director I would check it out. He gave me the phone number of the ambassador who was preparing to leave Trinidad, and what I heard from him was reassuring. It was an enjoyable assignment, the ambassador told me, and he was resigning only because his business, back home in Chicago, needed his attention. With that, my mind was settled, so I called the White House and said, okay, I would do it for a year or two.

While we were waiting for the State Department to complete its routine security checks on me, Ruth went out and brought home every book she could find on Trinidad and Tobago. Among the many things she learned was that the islands could be beastly hot, so, protesting that she had nothing to wear in a truly tropical climate, she made a shopping trip to Palm Beach to buy a whole new wardrobe.

Meanwhile, I began to worry about whether the life of a Caribbean ambassador was suited to my style. During a trip to Washington to talk with Ford's staff, I casually expressed concern that the rhythm of the islands might be too languid for me. I was accustomed to putting in long days and driving hard, I told them, and hoped the pace of Trinidad was not too slow for me. "I don't want to relax too much," I joked. "I might go a little crazy down there."

I thought very little about that comment, but apparently it registered with the Ford personnel chief. A few days later, I got another phone call from him. "We've come up with something that might be a little more your speed than Trinidad," he told me. "It's a major

administrative post that has just come open, and you may be the
man President Ford needs for the job.''

"Sounds interesting," I said. "What's the job?"

"The president wants you to be administrator of the GSA!"

He said it as if I should know what he was talking about, but I
didn't have the slightest idea. "What in the world is the GSA?" I
asked.

He explained it to me: the GSA is the Government Services
Administration, which is the primary business conglomerate agency
for the entire federal government. The director of the agency is
considered a major official, just below cabinet level, he said. The
man currently in the office, Art Sampson, was under fire for being
too political, and President Ford felt he needed to make a change.

So back to Washington I went, this time to learn more about the
GSA. If a tough challenge was what I wanted, Ford's staff assured
me, I would find all I could handle at the GSA. I finally told them
I would take the job, but only under the condition that I could
operate it without the intrusion of partisan politics, which I had
heard had been a problem with GSA administrators under previous
administrations.

"I will not accept the job," I spelled it out, "unless President
Ford tells me I will have one hundred percent authority to keep
politics out of it." They set up my appointment with President Ford,
and he agreed to those terms, so I returned to Clearwater to break
the news to Ruth.

When I got home, she was in Palm Beach on a final shopping trip
for her Trinidad wardrobe. I got home before she did and was
waiting for her when she walked through the door, arms loaded with
packages. "Forget those things and start shopping for a fur coat,"
I told her. "You and I are going to Washington."

I went up to Washington immediately—in December of 1975—
and moved into the Fairfax Hotel for a month, while Ruth settled
our affairs in Florida and bought a house and furniture in the Washington suburbs.

As soon as I arrived in town, I met with President Ford again at the White House, for a lengthy discussion of the GSA. He encouraged me to run the agency as much like a private business as possible, warning me that the requirement that I report to both the president and Congress would make the task more difficult. He again assured me I could operate on a strictly nonpolitical basis.

"I want you to run it as clean as a hound's tooth," he told me. "I've had all the flak I want from Jack Anderson [the columnist] about politicians finding jobs for their friends at GSA!"

"Are those my marching orders?" I asked.

"Yes, they are."

"Then I'll accept the appointment, Mr. President, and I assure you it will be run that way."

The GSA was a bureaucratic quagmire. That complex agency served many unrelated functions, ranging from managing the National Archives, to providing security for top government officials and buildings, to providing computer services for other agencies. It had 35,000 employees, controlled over 100 million square feet of office space, and ran 21 regional warehouses, which supplied the federal government with everything from paper clips to helicopters.

What made the GSA such a tough management job, however, was not its size and scope. It was the fact that all but 40 of its 35,000 employees worked under the provisions of the Civil Service Act, which meant that I had almost no latitude to reward them for exceptional productivity or punish them for exceptional nonproductivity. Consequently, things just didn't get done. The employees see GSA administrators—and United States presidents—come and go, and many learn that the safest way to survive political changes is to sit back, form committees, shuffle paper, and do as little as possible. For the staff member—and we had some—who aggressively made decisions and pushed ahead, there was great risk and very little credit.

Consequently, it was difficult for me to hire and fire, once I got below my top staff. We had a case in which an employee was caught stealing from a warehouse in Chicago, for instance. We couldn't fire him without going through a 90- to 180-day process; we couldn't even get him off the job in a temporary suspension for the first two weeks, so thick was the red tape of appeals and hearings necessary to deal with a case such as his.

I like the original concept of civil service. It was designed to keep politicians from jerking government employees around, abusing them on the job for their political activity—or lack of it. But the pendulum has swung far to the other end of the scale, and civil service now clearly damages efficiency in government agencies.

Before I went up to run the GSA, I never understood why it seemed so nearly impossible to run a federal department in a lean, cost-effective way. I still don't know some of the answers, but now I better appreciate the extent of the problem. In Washington, I met dozens of men and women who, like me, had left lucrative positions in private business to spend sixty-hour weeks working, with little thanks, at the job of trying to administer a federal department. Most, like me, were making sacrifices to be there, and most, like me, stayed frustrated half the time by the inability to streamline (let alone manage) the government system.

We did make progress, however, and my work in Washington, until I left in early 1977, was rewarding. Hundreds of our employees were just as frustrated by the system as I was and responded well to my nonpartisan management style. I also found that overall efficiency was sometimes best achieved by closing down an entire function of the agency and contracting it out to a private company. Over and over, we found that a private business—like security guards or janitorial services, for example—could usually do a better job, more cheaply, for us than we could do it with government employees.

This approach made more than a few people angry, especially the unions of which most of our employees were members. One day I got a call from a congressman who was on the GSA congressional oversight committee. He told me I was proceeding too fast with the privatization of agency functions and should slow down.

"But this approach is the right way to go," I insisted, "and you know it is!"

"Yeah, I know," he said. "But we're getting too much flak from the unions, so you're going to have to slow down anyway."

The last I knew he was still in the Congress, and I am sure, telling his constituents how much money he saved them in Washington.

One of the things I inherited at GSA was supervision of the Watergate papers. Most of them were kept on the top floor of the Executive Office Building, next to the White House, and it was the responsibility of the GSA to guard them. Because I was a Republican, the Democrats were always paranoid about my trying to do something inappropriate—I'm not sure what—with those papers.

A congressional committee called me into a hearing once to give me heat about not releasing some Watergate papers to them. I tried to explain my mandate for not doing what they wanted, but they were unwilling even to hear me out. As they persisted in berating me, I finally got hot and half-shouted into the microphone, "Listen, the only thing I am doing is following the orders I received from the Department of Justice, and I'm through listening to you guys." I got up and walked out of the hearing room. Those guys on the Hill were totally partisan on anything pertaining to Watergate, and to them, any Republican was a potential villain.

Nor did the Democrats cause all the problems. Scanning our payroll printout one day, I noticed that we were listing four salaries for men I had never seen at the GSA office. I asked someone who they were. "They work over at Vice-president Rockefeller's office" was the answer.

"Well, if they work for Rockefeller, why are they on our payroll?" I wanted to know.

No one knew the answer to that question; it was just one of those arrangements to which someone had agreed at some earlier time, they told me. So I instructed my payroll director to cut them off immediately. I figured that would smoke someone out, and it did.

Shortly afterward, I got a call from the vice-president, inviting me to join him for lunch at his office.

"Jack," he said genially, when the lunch dishes were cleared away, "apparently there's been a little misunderstanding over there about a few of my fellas that are carried on your payroll."

"I'm sorry, Mr. Rockefeller," I said, "but there is no misunderstanding. Those guys are on your staff, not mine, and I'm not going to carry them on my payroll."

"Aw, Jack, be reasonable," he argued, launching into a lengthy complaint about how the Congress would not allocate him adequate funds to run his office, and he had to find other ways to get his work done. "I need those guys, Jack," he pleaded. "You have such a big budget over there, what difference will a handful of staff members make to you? But I don't have any money for staff, Jack. Please try to understand my dilemma; if you upset our arrangement now, what am I going to do?"

He sounded so pitiful. I thought, *Good grief—this is the vice-president of the United States of America, sitting here begging me to manipulate my staff and payroll, just so he can have enough help to get his office work done. What kind of terrible shape this government bureaucracy must be in!*

I felt sorry for Rockefeller—it was obvious all he was trying to do was follow the traditional way of getting around his own payroll shortage. No way I could legally help him, though.

"I'm sorry, Mr. Rockefeller, but I can't help you. I understand your problem, but either those men come back over to GSA and work for us, or they don't get paid from our budget."

I maintained that position and never heard from the vice-president again. I still don't know where he found the money, but he apparently kept his staff members, because they never showed up at our place.

Perhaps the most interesting single incident of my Washington experience was the circumstances under which I departed.

When President Ford lost the election to Jimmy Carter in November of 1976, I prepared to leave Washington, along with the rest of the senior officials of the Ford administration.

I had hoped Ford would win the election, of course, and not just because he was a fellow Republican. I thought he had done a reasonably good job in a difficult situation, coming to the office in the aftermath of Watergate as he did. I thought then, as I do now, that he might have been an effective president in a full four-year term of his own.

I had another, more personal reason to wish for Ford's reelection: I wanted to continue my work as GSA administrator. Even with all the frustrations, I felt we were making progress in depoliticizing the agency and making it a more businesslike, efficient arm of the federal government. We had started some initiatives on which I hoped to follow through. If Ford lost, it was a foregone conclusion that I would automatically be replaced by a Carter appointee, just as cabinet officers would be. The GSA administrator had always been a partisan political choice.

So Ruth and I watched the election results that November with the knowledge that Ford's loss meant we would return to Florida and the life of private citizens once again.

Imagine my shock when I learned that the new president was considering asking me to stay on as a member of his administration. On December 16, as the Carter transition team set up shop in Washington and prepared for his inauguration, I received a telephone call from Bert Lance, one of Carter's closest advisers, who later became his budget director.

Lance asked me to meet with him, and I did, wondering what he might want. I was totally surprised by what he told me: "President Carter hears you run a good shop down there at GSA, and he wants to know if you would be interested in staying on."

I told Lance I might consider it, if we could keep things nonpolitical. I told him about my understanding with Ford and that I had an excellent staff that I would not want to see broken up for political reasons. I didn't want to be a token Republican in the Carter administration, I said, but if Carter truly wanted a nonpartisan operation, I was open to staying to run it.

When I talked with Ruth that night about our conversation, we were excited that we might be staying in Washington after all. We had come to enjoy living there and were pleased at the prospect that we might be staying in town after all.

In late January, only a week after the Carter inauguration, Lance called again, and I met with him and Hamilton Jordan, Carter's chief of staff. Jordan told me Carter had definitely decided to ask me to continue at GSA and that he would agree to my condition of a totally nonpolitical agency, at least for a six-month period. I told Jordan the appointment would have to be for at least a year, or I would be a lame duck, and that I would have to talk personally with the president before accepting, to make sure we understood each other.

No problem, Jordan said, and sure enough, one week later I was invited to the White House to meet with the president, alone. He told me I had been highly recommended by his fellow Democrats in the Senate and House and said he wanted the GSA run on a nonpolitical basis. I specifically told him that I considered the ability to choose my top staff to be part of that arrangement, and he agreed. He had also thought about my need for a guarantee of at least a one-year appointment, he said, and that was what he was offering.

When I left the president's office that day, we had a deal. The very next day a handwritten note on White House stationery was delivered to my office. It was from Carter: "To Jack Eckerd—I would like you to stay on as director of GSA. Bert Lance and Ham Jordan will consult with you on prospective internal organizational changes. My understanding is that you will be able to continue with this work for at least a year." It was signed "Jimmy C."

It was done. The next morning at 8:30 I met with my top staff and announced to them that I was staying. I said that my orders had come from the president himself and that I thought we could all march proudly to these orders. At noon, White House press secretary Jody Powell announced that I was staying; at 2:00 P.M., I met the press; and at 5:30 I conducted a conference call with all my regional administrators to tell them that they and my top staff were also staying on and that there would be no political influence applied to the agency, on direct orders of the president.

That was February 7. The pledge of no political pressure on the agency did not last even until the end of the day.

At 7:45 that evening, I got a call from Bert Lance, saying that he and Ham Jordan would be appointing a Democrat to the number-two spot in the agency. I told him to forget it. "No way," I said, "I have a personal assurance from the president." Lance didn't argue the point; he simply told me I would hear from Ham Jordan and hung up. Fifteen minutes later, I got a call from Jordan. He told me there had been a small mixup and that I must agree to accept their appointee as the deputy director, the agency's number-two spot.

"No way," I repeated. He said I would hear from the president.

Late that night, incredibly, I received a personal call from President Carter. I was at home; it was nearly 11:00 P.M., and Ruth answered the phone. "Good Lord," she whispered to me, "it must be something important! The president wants to talk with you!"

I took the phone.

"Jack?" Carter greeted me.

"Yessir."

He paused. "I'm embarrassed to call you, but I've got a problem."

"What is it, Mr. President?"

"Unknown to me, Jack, Ham Jordan made a promise to Tip O'Neill, and now I have to live up to it. He has promised Tip that one of his friends, Bob Griffin, would be named deputy director of the GSA. I knew nothing about this before I talked with you, but Tip now insists that Griffin must have that job."

I couldn't believe what I was hearing. "Now wait just a minute, Mr. President," I objected. "That's not our deal!"

"I know that, I know that," he interrupted, "but I had nothing to do with it. I'm just in a box, and I don't see any way out."

I said, "Mr. President, there must be ten jobs at that same level

open around town right now. Why is Tip O'Neill making a particular issue out of this one? I realize Griffin is his friend, but he could
make the same money, with the same status, somewhere else.''

Carter seemed frustrated by my resistance. ''I understand that,
Jack, but I've already met with Tip and Griffin, and they are pretty
determined about this. Besides, Griffin seems to me to be a pretty
capable fellow. I understand he works for you now.''

''I know, Mr. President,'' I said. ''I agree that Griffin is a knowledgeable person, but I'll tell you this: he is not capable of being and
is not going to be my deputy administrator. Besides, I've got the
best deputy administrator in Washington—Robbie Robinson—already aboard.''

''I'm sorry, Jack,'' Carter insisted, ''but I need Tip's help over
there on the Hill.''

It was a standoff. ''I'm sorry, too, Mr. President—when do you
want my resignation?''

But Carter would have none of that. ''No, no, Jack; that's not
what we want. Just think it over for a couple of days and come down
to the White House, and we'll talk about it.''

When we met in his office two days later, it was obvious that
there would be no compromise. Carter repeated to me that his staff
had committed to Tip, and he felt he must live up to it. It hurt him,
he said, not to be able also to honor his commitment to me. I
reminded him that he couldn't do both and that his decision would
put me in an untenable position. ''When would you like my resignation, Mr. President?'' I concluded.

''At your convenience,'' he replied quietly.

''Mr. President,'' I said, ''do you know what really chews me up
about this?''

''No, what is it?''

''What chews me up is the fact that here you are, the leader of the
free world, just coming into office, with all sorts of really important
things on your mind, and here you are spending hours and hours on
something like this, worrying about a second-level job in the GSA,

trying personally to work all this out to my satisfaction and Tip O'Neill's satisfaction. I'm really appalled that you've wasted so much time on us, Mr. President.''

"Well, Jack,'' he answered, ''that's my job.''

Within two days, I received another of Carter's handwritten notes, this one informing me that Griffin would be appointed deputy administrator the next Monday. I called him immediately to explain that the president did not have the legal authority to make this particular appointment; only the administrator of the GSA could do that, and I could not in good conscience do so.

My only honorable course was to resign, I told him, and two days later I did so. My deputy administrator and his chief assistant resigned with me. It was February 14, and as I began cleaning out my desk, my secretary stepped into the office to tell me the GSA staff was already referring to the episode as the Valentine Day Massacre.

The next day, President Carter appointed Griffin as acting administrator of the GSA. I had lasted less than a month in the ''nonpolitical'' Carter administration, and it was all so unnecessary. President Carter came to Washington proclaiming that he didn't owe the Democratic party anything. And he didn't. But the first time he had a showdown with Tip O'Neill, President Carter blinked!

I kept only one memento of that period in Washington. It is a framed photo that President Ford sent me of my farewell ceremony in the Oval Office. Ford inscribed the photo: ''To Jack Eckerd, the man who ran the GSA 'as clean as a hound's tooth.' ''

19

Charles Paul Conn

Though Jack and Ruth Eckerd persistently avoid discussing the details of their personal finances, their philanthropic activities are well known in Florida. People who give away literally tens of millions of dollars generally have trouble keeping other people from knowing about it.

The oldest and most significant recipient of the couple's largesse is a foundation they established to help troubled children and teenagers. The foundation, called Eckerd Family Youth Alternatives, Inc., began in 1968 and has become a major operation, with 600 employees and an annual budget of $20 million.

The primary function of the foundation is to operate "wilderness camps" to which emotionally troubled young people go for a period of one to two years. For these youngsters, aged ten to fifteen, the camps are typically an alternative to institutionalization, and the track record of the program shows an extraordinary success rate in returning them to mainstream situations.

In the Eckerd system, a social unit is made up of two teacher-counselors and ten children. These groups of twelve live together in a year-round, permanent campsite. They construct their own shelter, cut their wood for campfires and cooking, repair their own equipment, and generally manage their own group activity. Each camp includes five such groups, plus a transitional classroom of six to ten campers, and is located in a rural or wilderness area of Florida, North Carolina, Vermont, Rhode Island, or New Hampshire, on a remote tract of land owned or leased by the foundation.

The program is one-of-a-kind and has been acclaimed by social workers, juvenile-court officials, and educators as an innovative and well-managed solution to the problem of children who for various reasons cannot function well in ordinary settings. Eckerd says that the idea for the camps was borrowed from a similar operation in Texas.

Since the first camp was opened in 1968, over 5,000 children have been helped by the program. Eckerd takes great personal interest in the camps and the individual children. "We give a second chance to a child who may have grown up in an unsatisfactory home background," he said. "Most children can't tell one bug or flower from another and don't know how to paddle a canoe, but these kids can. We take them out of their surroundings, where they've often been told they're no good, and we spend a year with them, teaching them some important values."

The wilderness camps seem to be the concern that gets most of Eckerd's attention, but there is another charitable cause for which he is much more widely known: Eckerd College. The college, a liberal-arts institution in St. Petersburg, was formerly Florida Presbyterian College, but in 1972 changed its name to show appreciation for the Eckerds' generosity. The amount of money the Eckerds have given to the school over the years is not publicly known. Eckerd himself will not reveal the exact amount, nor will the college.

His involvement with the school began long before it bore his name. As a result of his involvement with other Presbyterian activities, he was asked to serve on the board of the college in the mid-1960s and gradually became an influential leader of the board, apparently more by virtue of his general force of personality than by any initiative on his part. When the college faltered financially in 1971, almost going bankrupt, he stepped in and secured its future with a major pledge that was announced to be the single largest gift ever made to a college or university in Florida. A year later, the school sought to broaden its public appeal by dropping its denominational label and struck upon the Eckerd name as a way of doing so. Eckerd himself thought it a good idea at the time for two reasons: First, some students said their friends teased them about going to a Bible college—which it was not. Second, a large gift from a hard-nosed businessman would convince other wealthy individuals and corporations that Florida Presbyterian College was worthy of their support too.

It didn't work. The increased support turned into less support. Too many potential supporters apparently thought it was a good college, but thought Jack Eckerd was standing in the wings to take care of all its needs. But the reasoning seemed sound in 1972, and the school became officially "Eckerd College."

His involvement with Eckerd College did not end there. In 1977, when he returned from Washington and his stint at the GSA, Eckerd found the school facing a serious leadership crisis and agreed to assume control of the college as interim president, until the spot could be filled permanently. For eight months, he wrestled with the daily operation of the ailing school, and when he left it in the hands of its new president, it was on its way to full recovery. Its enrollment, which had dropped to a low of about 700 students, is today back to a healthy 1,200 level.

After leaving the president's office, Eckerd served as chairman of the board. In recent years he has not been actively involved in the school's affairs, although its vice-president for development says, "His support still comes in."

Another recipient of Eckerd generosity is the arts community in the Tampa Bay area. Here again, the numbers are not available, but the suspicion is that they are large indeed, since the board of the

Performing Arts Center and Theatre (PACT) in Clearwater saw fit to give the name "Ruth Eckerd Hall" to its spectacular, $15 million performing arts center, which was completed in late 1983.

Quizzed about the amount of the Eckerds' contributions to the arts center, PACT officials respond that the Eckerds have requested the size of their gifts not be disclosed. "Let me put it this way," a PACT attorney told the local press, "if there were an archway of stones and the people involved with this operation were the stones, then the Eckerds would be the center or keystone."

No part of the Florida population is further removed from the glitter of Ruth Eckerd Hall than the prisoners who are inmates in the state's penal system, but that, too, is an important part of Eckerd's life today. His involvement in prisons and penal reform occupies much of his time and fits neatly both his religious inclinations and his political philosophy.

The Eckerd Foundation contracts with the state of Florida for the operation of the state's juvenile detention center in Okeechobee, Florida. The center is a full-scale juvenile prison, with some 300 residents serving sentences for crimes ranging from simple truancy to manslaughter. The foundation has accepted the responsibility of operating the facility, primarily for the purpose of demonstrating the ability of a private organization to operate with greater efficiency than a government agency, secondarily to allow Eckerd himself to spend his personal resources, in a quiet way, to improve the quality of life for the juveniles incarcerated there.

Says Eckerd: "As far as I know, Okeechobee is the only place in the country run this way. We run it, the state sets the budget, we hire and fire. There is no other juvenile prison of similar size that is operated by a private agency, and we want to show the private sector can do it better and cheaper."

Eckerd is also chairman of an organization called PRIDE (Prison Rehabilitative Industries and Diversified Enterprises, Inc.), which was set up by the state as a private agency to run its prison industries. Governor Bob Graham called upon Eckerd to head up this innovative operation, and he does so with enthusiasm, since it combines two of his favorite themes: prison reform and the privatization of government functions.

PRIDE is responsible for the management of industries in each of the state's prisons, producing an annual business volume of about $40 million. The agency uses inmate labor to operate various industries at a profit, then pays some money back to the prisoners, some to the state, and also some to the victims of the crimes. Eckerd says, "This program gives the prisoners a chance to make something of themselves and even allows restitution payments to victims."

Eckerd is eager to explain that the work of PRIDE is making an important point about the superior efficiency of the private sector: "The first industry we took over was a printing plant up in Zephyrhills. It was doing about $700,000 per year. This year it will do over twice that much business at a healthy profit. When the state was running it, if they ran out of a particular type of paper, they had to put out bids, wait thirty days, and spend several more weeks buying a thousand dollars' worth of paper. Now, our buyer is on the phone that day, places an order, and the next day a delivery truck backs up to our door, and the presses keep rolling. That's one reason why the private sector can do certain functions and provide certain services better than government can. The department of corrections simply had too many bureaucratic restrictions to operate efficiently. It wasn't their fault."

In 1986, Eckerd turned his political experience toward another cause—prohibiting casinos from operating in the state of Florida.

The strip of posh resort hotels along Miami Beach and the high level of tourism in the state generally have long made Florida a favorite target for the operators of gambling casinos. A group of investors who favor casino gambling succeeded in getting a referendum placed on the ballot in the November, 1986, election; it would have allowed counties to approve casino gambling for hotels with more than 500 rooms.

Eckerd led a statewide organization called No Casinos of Florida, Inc., which raised a more than $2 million campaign budget to urge citizens to vote no on the casino referendum. "When I heard of this on the ballot," he says, "I was willing to play a leading role against it, because I think it would be the worst thing that could happen to the state of Florida. I want to see this state remain a place my children and grandchildren can be proud to call home.

"This is not a moral issue. It has nothing to do with my personal view of most gambling being an evil. It has to do with the disastrous impact the casino industry would have on the quality of life in this state. I was assured by the political leaders who asked me to lead No Casinos, Inc., that I could do it without any political games being played, and that's the way it was done. We put together a team of Republicans, Democrats, whites, Hispanics and blacks, Catholics, Protestants, and Jews, senior citizens, young families, law-enforcement officers, political leaders and college folks—every group and faction in this state was part of the effort.

"The hard work paid off. We won sixty-eight percent of the statewide vote, with over two million people saying no to casinos in Florida. One of the most remarkable outcomes of the election was that we carried sixty-six out of sixty-seven counties in the state, losing only Dade County (Miami), and that by the narrow margin of fifty-two to forty-eight percent. It was an emphatic statement that the people of Florida do not want casinos in their state, now or ever."

20

Les Smout

Les Smout currently serves as chief financial adviser to Jack Eckerd, both for his personal affairs and for his various nonprofit organizations. He was previously vice-president for finance at Eckerd College, where he had worked for ten years before resigning to join Jack Eckerd's personal staff.

Mr. Eckerd was already on the board at Florida Presbyterian when I went there as internal auditor in 1967. I saw him work as a board member for over ten years, and briefly as interim president. On the board, he was a very straightforward, no-nonsense kind of guy. He asked tough questions. He never wanted to waste time. He would just sit there and listen, but when he said something, everybody paid close attention.

He came to the school as interim president, right after leaving the GSA. Like everybody else, I held him in awe. We were all pleased when we learned he might become interim president, but I was afraid that when he had finished with that, he might feel that he couldn't serve as chairman of the board, and I felt the chairmanship was where we needed him most. We ended up getting the best of both worlds—he bailed us out as interim president, then stayed on for the next three years as chairman of the board.

When he got there, the school was in a crisis situation. The finance committee was having weekly meetings on Monday nights, trying to find new places to cut the budget. We were in dire hardship: utility costs had gone straight up; we had cut the dickens out of the physical plant budget; we had fallen from 1,100 students down to 825, in a period of five years.

I knew the school was a high priority to him at that time, and the place was coming apart at the seams. That's why he came. I don't think he ever enjoyed it; but if he had not stepped in, I believe the college would have gone down the drain, if not the summer of 1977, then by the summer of 1978. What he brought, mostly, was some stability and credibility; the financial community took heart and regained confidence when he came on as president.

His most unique feature is that he can take a topic that he knows basically nothing about, hear a presentation on it, ask some questions, probe, ask some more questions, and analyze the situation correctly. He has the uncanny ability to ask the right questions. I know some of the numbers around here in greater detail than he does, but he has a better grasp of the overall picture than I do.

I enjoy watching him work. The guy just sits there and asks questions, and you can almost hear the wheels turn in his mind. He can cut through to the heart of a matter faster than anyone I've ever seen. I tell people who come to work for him, "If you don't know the answer to something he asks you, you better tell him you don't know, then go check it out, and get back to him. Don't try to snow the old man. He usually catches you at it, and when he does, he will have a piece of your hide!"

21

When I returned from Washington, I hardly even considered going back to the corporation on an active basis. It was clear to me that the part of my life devoted to leading the Eckerd drugstore business was over, and I began looking for other mountains to climb.

There were plenty of jobs from which to choose—for a man with an appetite for hard work and experience in administration, there is never a shortage of causes to espouse in the not-for-profit sector. I found that my calendar stayed as busy and my desk as full as it had when I worked in business or politics.

My challenge was not to find things to do, but to select carefully those movements in which to invest my time, energy, and resources. Over the past several years, I have taken seriously the need to get involved only in those causes that can make a significant difference in some permanent way. I have found such causes and plunged into them. I have never felt comfortable as a mere "checkbook philanthropist."

Through the late seventies and the eighties, with time out for the 1978 gubernatorial race, I worked hard at such causes. I was enjoying what must have seemed to others a nearly perfect life. Certainly the pieces were in place. I could tick them off almost as if from a checklist of the things that ought to add up to the perfect life:

great marriage and a loving family; excellent health; a successful career to look back on; plenty of money; good friendships, developed over the years in politics and business; a good reputation; meaningful work to do.

What more could a person possibly expect from life?

I had everything that I could reasonably want; still, for some reason I was not content. I had sense enough to know something was missing. I talked with a couple of close friends about my lack of satisfaction, and they obviously wondered what was wrong with me. They told me I should feel great about my life, that I should be the most contented man in town. No one need feel sorry for Jack Eckerd—that's for sure.

What I was feeling was spiritual restlessness.

I didn't recognize it as such, because I had very little background in spiritual matters. I knew that a vague discontent, a restlessness, had been building inside me for many years, but only later did I recognize it for what it was—the emptiness of a man who does not have a meaningful personal relationship with God.

It was not that I was a heathen. I had been a church member for many years, a Presbyterian of the conventional sort. Ruth and I had become Presbyterians soon after we married and have faithfully supported our congregation and its needs.

As a child growing up, I called myself a Methodist, although I actually had very little religious training at all. My parents took us to church regularly, but we had no religious life in the home. I don't recall either my father or mother taking much personal interest in religion; as most families do, we went through the formalities. We were good casual Christians.

Ruth was born and raised a Baptist. When we were married and she moved from Tampa to join me at our new home in Clearwater, it took her away from her church. After we moved into the new neighborhood, the question arose of where we would attend church. "One thing for sure," I declared, "we are not going to have one of those families in which I am a Methodist and you are a Baptist. That's out." She agreed heartily.

A neighbor told us there was a good Presbyterian church only a few blocks away, so we visited the service one Sunday morning. We enjoyed the sermon that morning, and the people were friendly, so we joined. That was how we became Presbyterians.

We were good church members, especially Ruth, and I had no complaints about the church over the years. After two or three years, I was asked to serve on the board of deacons and did so. I found no spiritual nourishment in that at all—just constant meetings in which we hassled with the budget and debated whether we should spend a few hundred bucks to fix the roof. I thought the staff should handle things like that, and we should be talking about our kids' religious upbringing and what we could do to help people outside the church. So after my first term was up, I didn't stay on the board.

I would describe my church attendance as semiregular. If a good tennis match came along on Sunday morning, I was quick to tell Ruth, "You take the kids to church; I need to get out and get some exercise." When I went, I sometimes sat in the pew and questioned whether I had wasted an hour. All in all, I think I was a pretty typical businessman in that regard.

But gradually, as my restless feeling about life grew, I came to suspect that it was a religiously based hunger of some sort, some spiritual need that conventional church membership did not meet. I came to realize that I was getting nothing from my faith and wondered how I might go about changing that.

At that point in my life, several unrelated events occurred, the combination of which changed my life in a permanent way. I never had a dramatic single experience of spiritual conversion, in which I went from a desperately evil man into a saint. I have heard many stories of spiritual change that include some specific moment of tears and repentance, and I do not doubt those stories at all, but that is not what happened to me.

What *did* happen to me is just as miraculous, however. Gradually, over a period of a year or two, God led me into a personal relationship with Him, and the result is that I am a different person from the man I was before I knew God in this way. I now understand and accept the authority of Jesus Christ in my life, and that isn't easy for a hard-driving business leader who is in the habit of making his own decisions.

One of the catalysts in my spiritual awakening was my next-door neighbor in Clearwater, a man named Vic Wickman. Vic was a successful insurance agent. Several years earlier, a drinking problem had damaged his family life and had nearly blown his marriage apart. A friend of Vic's had shared the gospel with him, and in the process Vic had become a born-again Christian. Now his life seemed fully restored, and his business and personal affairs had rebounded. I did not know him well, but considered him to be a good neighbor.

Vic began conducting a Bible study in his home, every Thursday morning, at 6:30. A Bible study in one's home was an unfamiliar concept to me, itself, but to have it at that time of day seemed ridiculous. *Who would ever go to a man's house at that time of morning to talk about religion?* I wondered.

I have always been an early riser, and it was my custom to walk or jog around the neighborhood early every weekday morning. On Thursdays, I began to notice a growing number of cars outside Vic's house. On some days, there would be literally dozens of cars, lined along the curb up and down our block.

On one such morning, after my walk, I commented to Ruth as we drank our coffee, "I wonder what Vic is pitching to those kooks, every Thursday morning, that has so many of them showing up at six-thirty in the morning?"

"Maybe you should stop by some morning and find out," she suggested.

I didn't intend to do that, but curiosity got the upper hand, and one Thursday morning soon afterward, I showed up at Vic's door. I went into his large living room, quietly found a seat, and looked around at the seventy or eighty men who were there. They didn't look like kooks; they were mostly young and middle-aged professional men and businessmen, with a few retirees included.

I listened to what Vic was saying that morning, and there was nothing particularly exotic or provocative about it. He sat on a stool in front of the crowd, with a Bible in his hand, and led us in a discussion of a selection of Scriptures. It was simple and down-to-earth, and it was interesting, so I decided to come back the next week.

My visits became a regular thing. No one put any heat on me to come back or even paid much attention to me, for that matter. There were a few people there I knew, but none of them, including Vic, made a big deal out of my showing up. I had been somewhat reluctant to go, for fear of being a conspicuous outsider in such a religious group, afraid someone might make a move on me to join something or pray or whatever. But nothing like that happened. It was very low key, just a group of men meeting to read the Bible and discuss it, and I found it comfortable to return.

Before then, I had occasionally tried to read the Bible, but I had always read a few pages and given up. Vic would read a Scripture, then give an explanation for the reasons it was written and how it applied to our real-life situations. Suddenly, the Bible began to make sense to me. Another thing different about those morning sessions was that other people would chime in as Vic taught.

These were not preachers—they were secular men just like me. But they would tell about their experiences or the experiences of a brother or a friend. It got very personal. I was seeing, probably for the first time, the practical application of the Bible to a person's life, and that was fascinating to me. I now know it is the most practical book in the world, if one knows how to apply it, but at the time I had always regarded the Bible as very theoretical and detached from my ordinary life.

I began to read the Bible a lot—not just with that group of men on Thursday mornings, but every day, myself, and I began to ask God to help me understand it and apply it. When I did that, for the first time in my life, I realized that I believed Someone was actually hearing my prayer.

Vic Wickman was not the only person who was instrumental in pointing me toward Christ. Another was Bill Glass, the former football player who had been an all-pro with the NFL's Cleveland Browns. When his career on the football field ended, Glass began a full-time ministry to prisoners, which coincided with my interest in Florida's penal system.

I accepted an invitation to attend a weekend seminar conducted by Glass. It was in Milledgeville, Georgia, where several hundred Christian businessmen met to share testimonies and discuss ways to spread God's word in prisons. That weekend, I saw another version of what I was seeing in Vic's Bible study—the excitement of Christianity and the potential it had to change lives. The weekend made a major impact on my attitude toward becoming a Christian myself.

Later, Bill Glass visited me at my office in Clearwater. We spent a lot of time talking about prisons and penal reform, but the subject inevitably turned to that of Christian commitment, and Glass was very patient and skillful in explaining his faith to me. As he said good-bye he gave me his personal Bible as a gift—I still use it in my devotions and Bible study.

About this time I met Chuck Colson, who would be the single most influential person to me in my development as a Christian disciple.

I had an active interest in prison reform—still do—as a result of my work with the wilderness camps for troubled kids and with the prison industries of the state of Florida. While watching television one Sunday afternoon, I saw Chuck Colson appear on a talk show with William F. Buckley. The topic was penal reform; Colson was arguing for a completely changed concept of prisons and how we use them. His basic point was that nonviolent, nondangerous criminals should be made to do restitution for their crimes, rather than being locked up in high-security prisons.

Colson made sense; even Buckley concurred. I didn't know anything about him at the time, except that he had been on Nixon's staff during the Watergate days and that he had been to prison as a result of that scandal. I had read somewhere about his religious conversion, but had thought little of it, dismissing it as a publicity stunt to get a lighter sentence or to set himself up for parole. I had not given Colson or his conversion story much thought, one way or the other, but he got my attention on the Buckley show that afternoon. *This guy,* I figured, *is one smart cookie; I would like to talk with him about prison reform.*

So I called Colson, a month or so later, and he remembered who I was. I had been in Philadelphia when Nixon announced revenue sharing, and Colson and I had chatted briefly then. Plus I had met him on another, more recent occasion, up in North Carolina. I asked Colson to come by Clearwater—I had heard he traveled often to this part of Florida—to talk with me and my staff about prison reform. When we met, I asked him, "What can we do to help solve the prison problem right here in Florida?"

He had an idea. "There is a package of reform legislation, already almost written and ready to go, which we can present to the Florida legislature. If we could work together, you and me and Jim Smith [the attorney general], and go on a 'campaign swing' around the state of Florida, I believe we could sell that legislative package, and if we could, it would make a major impact on the prison system in this state."

That sounded like my kind of action. "Get us a plane," Colson suggested. "And use your contacts to line up all the heavy hitters in every major city—politicians, media people, law-enforcement officials—and we'll hit about three cities each day, just barnstorm this whole state."

We did just that, and it was a successful effort. The legislature passed the package of prison reforms we were pushing, and it made a big difference in Florida. But an important by-product of that trip, for me personally, was that I developed a good friendship with Colson, and we stayed in touch fairly regularly after that.

Colson sent me books to read. I read his own testimony, of course, in his book *Born Again*, as well as several other things he sent me, and in our discussions about those books and spiritual things in general, I grew closer and closer to a sense that I could know God for myself in a way that I previously had not.

Colson had a way of challenging me without pushing me. He is a very forthright person; he doesn't mince words when something is important to him. But at the same time, he never tried to shove religion down my throat. I knew he was interested in my spiritual condition; I knew he wanted to see me make a public confession of faith in Christ, but I never had the feeling he was one of those Christian scalp hunters, out to add me to his "saved" list.

I had bumped into people like that before, and they turned me off. Like many secular businessmen, I had learned to put my hand over my wallet when people started talking to me about God. One example was a fellow whom I had met at Vic Wickman's Bible study. This guy wasn't a regular at Vic's; he just happened to be there one morning, and we had met casually.

He called the office soon after, and asked if he could come see me. "Sure," I said, "come on by." He made me uneasy from the moment he arrived. It was obvious he had only one thing on his mind—getting Jack Eckerd "saved." He said to me when he came into my office, "Brother Eckerd, I can see by your eyes that I can do something for you, because you're my brother!"

After only about two or three minutes of conversation, he asked, "Would you mind getting down on your knees and letting me pray with you?" Well, sure I minded, but I wasn't going to tell the guy he couldn't pray, so we knelt on the carpet, and he prayed a little prayer. When we got to our feet, he told me what a great guy I was and how he was going to help me find the Lord. He would be back, he said.

He called again in a few days and asked to borrow some money. I told him no, and I never heard from him again. The tragedy of that episode is that it has happened so often, in one form or another, to so many people who have been totally turned off by it and as a result are cynical about religious people generally.

Chuck Colson didn't crowd me, and when we talked about my spiritual condition, it was usually at my initiative rather than his. When we got into the subject, though, he was a tough and hard-nosed advocate of the born-again experience. He knew what he was talking about, and he didn't yield an inch.

Once, during a phone conversation, he drew the parallel between

Watergate and the resurrection of Christ: "There were actually eleven of us in the White House who knew what was going on. When that thing broke, three out of the eleven squealed, went to the Justice Department, and threw themselves on the mercy of the court.

"Compare that to the life of Christ," he said. "As many as five hundred people actually saw Him after He was resurrected. During the next hundred years, practically all of them were thrown in jail, deserted by their families, tortured, even killed for being His followers, and not a one of them ever changed his story. Do you think that's a coincidence? It must have been real, Jack—not just real, but an overpowering thing in every one of their lives."

I thought about that for about a week, and called him back. "You got me cornered, Chuck."

For those people who want me to tell them when and how I was born again, my answer is, "I don't know—it didn't happen overnight." Maybe my lack of a dramatic conversion prayer will bother some people—maybe it will reassure some, too, who are like me. But that's the way it was.

When Chuck and I were talking that day about Watergate, he got a little irritated with my indecisiveness. "The problem with you, Jack," he said, "is that you won't decide whether to really buy into this thing. You keep sitting on the fence. You're supposed to be one of these hot-shot business guys who makes fast decisions; when are you going to make up your mind on the most important decision you'll ever make?"

Chuck had a way of getting my attention.

Suddenly it was clear that Jesus took on my sins and the sins of others, and by doing this he purchased eternal life for us. My eternal life was not the result of what I had done for Him, but what Christ had done for me when He died on the cross. I realized that, at some point, I had to pray in faith and accept Christ's death for my sins, rather than trusting in my own deeds to make me God's child. I had spent enough time thinking about it and talking about it. I made a decision to trust Him, and I have never been "on the fence," intellectually or emotionally, since that time. But don't ask me the day, week, or month.

Things have changed in my life since 1982. I have a peace of mind I never had in seventy years; I have a confidence that I can seek personal guidance from God, in the Bible, and in prayer. In fact, I get a great satisfaction from prayer that I never got before, a satisfaction that comes from the feeling that God really listens. I used to pray when I went to bed at night, but I'm not sure it had much significance, because I don't think I ever really thought of myself as talking *with* God when I prayed. I think it was a matter of feeling that everyone should pray every day, so I went through the motions.

Prayer works. By that, I mean it is more than just psyching yourself up; it works in the sense that it changes things as God hears our prayers and answers them. I don't pretend to know *how* it works, but I know it does. I don't pretend that God always uses my timing in answering prayer, but He answers. I pray for things I need, sure, and things I want to see happen. But I also find myself praying as I drive to work, thanking God for things I've always taken for granted.

My Bible reading is different, too. I read three or four chapters a day and use the Navigators' "Daily Walk" to read through the Bible in a year. That keeps me in line and reduces my tendency to procrastinate.

Another thing that is new to me is a desire to see other people discover the relationship with Christ that I have found. I still don't know exactly how to go about this. I don't walk up to my friends and start quoting Scriptures to them, but I am trying to let my life be a witness. When they have things in their lives they need help with, that is the time I want to share with them. I still don't have the answers about how best to share Christ with one's friends; I think everybody has to work that out for himself.

It would be foolish for me to be impatient when the people I love do not take to this as fast as I would like. I try to be understanding and patient, because I know how long it took for God to get through to me.

22

Chuck Colson

Chuck Colson was an attorney in the Nixon White House who was involved in the Watergate scandal, in 1973. After serving a brief prison sentence on charges related to Watergate, he began a professional writing and speaking career as well as Prison Fellowship Ministries, a Washington, D.C., based Christian organization that seeks to help prisoners and their families, as well as work for reforms in the criminal-justice system.

I remember meeting Jack Eckerd in Highlands, North Carolina, in the summer of 1982. Highlands is a popular summer resort for affluent Floridians, and Jack has a house up there. I was in Highlands to speak at a Christian businessman's dinner one evening and went to a reception the afternoon before. I had heard Eckerd would be there and was a bit apprehensive about what he would be like— I thought he wouldn't be very approachable. I had tried to call his office once and hadn't been able to get through.

At the reception, I saw Eckerd mingling in the crowd, and soon afterward he walked up to me and said, "You're Chuck Colson; I want to meet you; I saw you on TV with Bill Buckley, and you make more sense than anybody I ever listened to.'' Just like that. I was impressed by his direct manner, and we sat down at a table and had a good chat about the issues I had discussed on that television show.

Eckerd showed up at the dinner. I gave an evangelistic ''hard sell'' that night. I really laid the gospel on those people and told them they needed to pray that very night—which is rather more direct than I usually am in a situation like that. I really gave the crowd no middle ground; I told them they had to make a personal choice about Jesus Christ.

I remember looking at Eckerd while I was speaking. He has extraordinary eyes; when he's looking at you, it's hard to look away. He was sitting in the middle of the room, and it seemed his eyes were fixed on me. I like eye contact when I'm speaking, of course, but this was almost more than was comfortable, so I would look away and then would be drawn back. He was so intense.

When dinner was over and people were standing around, he took off like a shot. I think he was the first person to leave. At the door, he turned and waved at me across the room. ''So long, Chuck,'' he said with a big smile. I answered jokingly, ''You don't have to hurry, Jack, we're not raising money!'' After he left, I expected never to see him again; I thought I had probably overkilled in my speech and had turned him off—despite his smile.

A couple of weeks later, I got a call from his secretary, saying he would like to visit with me, if I could come to Clearwater. So one day I went by his office and spent a couple of hours with him and his entire staff, talking about reforming the prison system in Florida, which was in a real mess. I was very much impressed with Jack. I found him much more approachable and down-to-earth than I expected. He was salty and interesting. But mostly I saw that he really cared about the criminal justice system in his state, about the conditions in which the people lived.

The Florida prison system was in chaos. They were increasing the inmate population at the rate of 400 new people per month, proposing $350 million in new prisons, and already had experienced an almost tenfold increase in the corrections budget in ten years, from

$42 million to $400 million a year. People in Florida were throwing up their hands in despair.

That day in Clearwater, I told Jack I thought we could draw up legislation that would help solve Florida's problems. His eyes brightened. He said, "Okay, let's get some people together, write it up, tour the state, and see if we can't sell it." He organized meetings across Florida, put a team of political leaders together, and we got in his Learjet and took off.

At every single meeting on that trip, Eckerd introduced me, and the introduction was always the same. He would tell the audience how he had met me and then would say, "So I want to introduce to you my friend Chuck Colson. He's born again; I'm not; but I wish I were." It was the same every time.

The first time, I thought he was joking, but the second time, his introduction seemed almost plaintive, with almost a cry for help in his voice, a cry I think only I could hear.

After one of these introductions, when we were back on the plane, I said, "Jack, you said something about wishing you were born again. Do you know what that means?" "Sure, I think so," he answered. "I heard you speak in Highlands."

We stayed in touch after that trip, and I found occasions to explain the gospel to him. He would simply nod, smile, or respond in a non-committal fashion. He told me about his neighbor's Bible study, said it was interesting; it was obvious he was very impressed with this guy. But I gave him several openings and could never get him to respond.

After a while, I decided there must be something in his life he wouldn't give up. I have discovered that most people do not have intellectual objections to the gospel; they have moral objections. They believe it; they just don't want to do what it requires. My first suspicion was that Jack must have a girl friend. That is not uncommon, for a man like him, a big shot, lots of money, drives a Porsche— he could have a lot of women.

So I asked him. I figured I needed to push this guy, find out what his problem was. I said, "Jack, you're holding back; you must have something that's an obstacle to you. I don't want to be personal, but do you have a girl friend?''

He seemed horrified at the thought. ''Oh no, no! Nothing like that! I'm a very happily married man, Chuck.''

I could see that a girl friend was not the problem.

There were two phone conversations that were, I think, particularly significant during that year (1983). Once, I asked him, ''Jack, have you made a decision about Christ in your life?''

''No,'' he said.

I got a little annoyed, for some reason. I said, ''Well, Jack, you've been reading all these books. You know what the gospel is; why haven't you decided?''

He shrugged me off: ''Well, I'm looking at it; I'm thinking about it.''

That irritated me even more. I said, ''You businessmen really amaze me. Just about anything that comes along, you have to make decisions. You built hundreds of drugstores. You had to decide on locations for every one of them. You had to pick managers. You had to make deals. The one thing you could always do was to make a decision. Now it comes to the most important single question in your life, and you can't make a decision. You have a reputation for being tough and decisive and all that stuff. Baloney! You may as well quit reading about God and talking about God, until you've got the guts to make a decision about God!''

The other memorable conversation was when he called me and wanted to talk about the comparison between Watergate and the resurrection, which I had made in one of my books, *Loving God*.

''Boy, that's strong!'' he said. ''I don't see how anyone can argue with the resurrection of Christ; the evidence is just overwhelming!''

I said, ''Well, what does it mean to you?''

Jack: ''I believe it happened.''

''You mean you believe that Christ is the Son of God?''

''Sure, I do.''

"You believe what He said, that no man comes to the Father but through Him, that He is the way, the truth and life?"

"Absolutely."

"You believe the Bible?"

"I've read the whole thing from cover to cover, and I believe the whole thing."

"Jack," I told him, "if you believe that and you've asked God to help you to live by it, then you're a Christian; you're born again, right now!"

He protested, "But I haven't felt anything. I haven't had an experience, like you."

"You don't have to have an experience, Jack," I said. "You just pray, ask Jesus Christ to come into your life, and let Him know you trust Him. That's how it comes."

"Is that right?" he asked, and it sounded as if a light bulb had come on in his head. We had a little prayer over the phone, and I felt that Jack had broken through.

Within two months, I picked up a newspaper and saw that Eckerd had mounted a major campaign among his management team that had resulted in removing *Playboy* and *Penthouse* from the shelves of his stores. I called him and told him how great I thought that was. "I don't think a guy would do that unless Christ were leading in his life. Did you do that because you've become a Christian?" I asked.

"Why else do you think I would give away several million dollars a year in sales volume?" he shot back at me. "I did it because God just wouldn't let me off the hook."

That was the first time I knew of Jack Eckerd accepting the label *Christian*, and I knew then that his life was deeply and permanently changed.

Lots of evangelicals have a warped view; they feel there has to be a particular moment, a flood of tears, that sort of thing, for a person to become born again. But there are lots of people who pass from darkness to light, but they don't know precisely when the light came on. They know it's light, and it was once dark.

Jack Eckerd is that way. He is a totally different person. He was once a very impatient, demanding man. People who worked with him say this was one of the toughest, hardest-nosed businessmen you'll ever find, the kind who wouldn't give you twenty seconds for small talk and who was totally goal-oriented. Now he is a different guy. He's more relaxed. It is evident, in the time since I met him, how much more he is at peace with himself.

23

Now that I understand how God works in a person's life, I can look back over my seventy-plus years and make better sense of it than I ever could before.

In some ways, I feel almost as if I have been sleepwalking—I have been so unaware of the things of God that now seem so real around me. It's not that I was ever an overtly evil person; to the contrary, I have always tried to be "good" in the usual sense, and most of my friends would have told you I succeeded. I always worked hard to deal honestly with others and to be generous with those who were less fortunate than I was just as the majority of my friends and business acquaintances had done.

I don't think I was blatantly evil, in any sense. I was just an average person who didn't know what it meant to let God's Spirit work in my life. Since I had never experienced that, I had no basis for comparison, and I thought my life without God was the only kind of life there was. It was relatively late in life that I came to feel there was something missing.

Looking back to my early years as a young pilot, I now believe that there were times when God protected me for His own purposes. During the war, I was not scornful of religious things at all. I was no more or less sinful than most of the GIs of my acquaintance. God was just not a meaningful part of my life in any way. Vaguely, in the back of my mind, I did believe in a God and a hereafter, but I certainly didn't think about it very often. I made no attempt to communicate with God; I don't recall anyone around me who did.

The same thing could be said about every other stage of my life. God was not actively on my mind, although I realize now He was by my side, whether or not I recognized and acknowledged Him. Like many other businessmen who have made fortunes in the tens of millions, I have sometimes wondered why such good things happened to me. Of course, I could chalk up my success to hard work and sound business principles, and that had lots to do with it. You don't put together a major corporation just by luck and prayer—there were thirty years of sweat and sacrifice involved, and I don't want to diminish that.

On the other hand, any businessman who has been as successful as I am, if he has even an ounce of humility or honesty, will admit that he knows peers who are just as smart, have worked just as hard, have followed the same business principles, and somehow have enjoyed only a fraction of the material success.

Why me? the question remains. Timing, I have often answered: my success was so big because the timing was right. But that does not answer the question; it only rephrases it. Why was my timing so right? I now have an answer for that question, which I didn't have before. I now understand that the only way we can explain why things happened the way they did, in many cases, is to say simply that God willed it to be so.

To explain one's success by ascribing it to the hand of God is not easy to do for us pragmatic, hard-core businessmen. We find it difficult for two reasons. First, it is an explanation that doesn't stroke the individual's ego. The old-fashioned idea of self-reliance and hard work encourages us to take our chances in life, take our lumps when we lose, and then enjoy taking credit for our success when we win. To admit that the credit belongs to God and His goodness, more than to us and our ingenuity, is not a big boost to the ego.

For many successful men and women, it is our egos that God has trouble getting us to submit to Him. That part of Christian living may be more difficult to learn for successful people than for people whose luck has run out. I'm sure that was the case with me.

There is another reason we hesitate to ascribe our business and professional success to the hand of God: to do so requires us to place all that we own at His disposal. If He gave it to us, then we must be willing to give it back to Him and His kingdom, rather than hoarding it for ourselves, determined to keep every scrap until we die, then leave it to our children.

God has shown me, as I have prayed and read the Bible, that everything I have belongs to Him, and He expects me to make optimum use of it for the work He is doing in this world.

That does not mean God wants me to give it all away, right now, to whoever happens to ask for it. He expects me to use the same intelligence and analytical skills that helped me to make it in the first place. Nor am I talking merely of money. Most of us have many kinds of resources: energy, influence, management skills, insight into people, time, connections, reputation, and of course money. All that now belongs to God, and I take seriously my responsibility to use it all for Him, with the maximum possible effectiveness.

If there is anything I regret about my new relationship with Jesus Christ, it is only that it happened so late in my life. I lived seventy years without understanding how to be close to God, and if I worried about the wasted opportunities of those seventy years, it would drive me crazy. Fortunately, I have never been one to look back. I don't believe in wringing my hands over things that are past that I can do nothing about.

But there is one thing I *can* do at my age, and that is to leverage my resources, in the years I have, to their maximum use. Every day when I pray, I ask the Lord to show me how I can best leverage whatever resources I have for the work of His kingdom. Who was it who said he never saw a U-Haul trailer hitched to the back of a hearse? My resources are finite; I have only so much time, energy, or money, and I want to maximize every bit of it for God.

Sometimes that means giving it away, and sometimes that means investing it, so that I have additional resources again to leverage.

Now that I realize it all came from God anyway, I have a greater sense of responsibility about the way I use it.

Now that my formal association with the Eckerd Corporation has ended, I can reflect on the thirty-five years I spent with that company and find much of which to be proud.

I made a promise to myself when I made our first public stock offering—a promise that we would never adopt any policy or take any corporate action that we did not think was in the best interest of our customers, our stockholders, and our associates. I think we lived up to that promise.

The thing that pleases me most is that I was able to deliver on my promises to those people who believed in me from the beginning and who helped make Eckerd Drugs a great company. Every $1,000 investor in our original stock issue in 1961 was paid $158,000 for that stock in the buyout that occurred in 1986.

I also take great satisfaction in the way my business associates have fared over the years. Because I believe so strongly in employee stock ownership, I gave stock to each Eckerd associate in 1961, and between 1974 and 1981, I sold almost 2.5 million shares at under ten dollars a share to our associates. I am happy that, while I have prospered by the success of our company, thousands of other hard-working employees have prospered along with me.

Those things give me a great sense of satisfaction, but I have learned in recent years that succeeding in business, even when one tries to achieve it with a high degree of ethics and fairness, can ultimately become quite empty. No amount of success and no amount of civic duty has ever given me the personal fulfillment that I have found by submitting my life to Jesus Christ.

Assessing my business career, I can see that I was working for the Game. That was the source of my fulfillment—winning at the Game. And it was a great Game, that of beating the competition in an honest fight where the public renders the decision of who has won and lost. I got some of the greatest ''highs'' of my life by moving down to Florida, where all these large drugstore companies were already established, and coming up with a little different concept, a few new ideas, a great bunch of associates, and growing right past the others.

Winning at that Game was one of the delights of my life. It was more fun than fishing or playing tennis. I loved the Game, and I think the record shows I played it well; still it was not enough to fulfill me.

I am aware that anytime an individual says he has learned a new walk with God, he opens himself up to a certain amount of skepticism. I understand that, and I don't mind it. People might hear my testimony and say, "Well, Jack Eckerd spent all those years living fast and making money, and now that he is seventy, he suddenly gets religion. If Jesus is so real, why didn't Eckerd figure that out years ago?"

The only response I would have is this: I am telling you what happened to me. That's all. This is what took place in my life, and if it had happened earlier, I would have talked about it earlier. I greatly regret that I did not know God earlier in my life, and if I let myself look back at all the joy I missed by being so blind all those years, it would drive me crazy, so I won't do that.

I realize that I went through my life missing the best parts, but, thank God, I finally woke up, and now I intend to enjoy every day playing catch-up.

Would I have managed Eckerd Drugs differently had I been a Christian at the time? In some ways, yes, I think so. I think I may have pushed people too hard, expected my store managers to extend themselves too much, over too long a period of time, just because that is the way I like to work. I'm afraid the amount of work I asked from them made it less possible for them to have the fully rounded lives we all should have.

In the days when we were building so fast, I would occasionally get a letter from a wife of one of our managers, saying, "Mr. Eckerd, you shouldn't ask my husband to work so many hours. He's neglecting his family." I responded by saying that the payoff was coming for them, and that although his wife might not realize it, this was the best thing for them ultimately. I think my drive for the success of our company broke up a few marriages, and that definitely goes down as a big regret. It would have better served the Lord's purpose and the company's purpose if I had not asked my management people to work so many sixty- to eighty-hour weeks.

I don't spend any time dwelling on it, because there is nothing I can do about it, but if I were operating the company now, I would spend more time on the personal growth of the families of my associates.

My desire to see my employees prosper is not new; but now I know that's not enough. Such a perspective is what makes a Christian manager a better manager, all other things being equal—serving God opens him up to the broader range of the needs of his people.

Giving myself to Christ has made a difference in the way I think, the way I feel about other people, and the way I make decisions. Some people seem to be in direct communication with God about everyday things, and I am not that way. I don't get a scroll dropped in my lap every time I have a decision to make. But I definitely have lost the feeling that I am in complete control of my life; I know now that God is in charge, there has been a change of command. God has taken over the throne of my life; I'm no longer in the "catbird seat," and that is a big difference from the "old" Jack Eckerd.

I submit my game plan to the Lord and ask Him to somehow let me know if it is not in keeping with His plan to further the kingdom of God. The tough decisions are easier for me, now that I have learned to do this. I still have to decide, still have to go ahead and act. But I believe that if I am about to make a big mistake, somehow God will close the door and push me in a new direction.

With that prayer, I then move forward, while I try to stay alert to His signals. That is why I am so looking forward to the future—because it is a future in which God, not Jack Eckerd, is in charge.

24

An Eckerd Sampler

ON HIS REPUTATION FOR FRUGALITY: I don't like wasting money, of course, but more than that, I dislike being taken. When you pay three or four times more than it's worth for something, you're being taken, no matter whether or not you can afford it. I always fly coach, for example. I've tried flying first class, and it's just not worth it, so I fly coach. If I analyze it, I'll admit it seems silly for me not to fly first class, since it wouldn't make any difference to my net worth, one way or another. But the idea of paying a couple of hundred dollars to the airlines for a free drink and maybe better food is what I don't like. It's value that I look for—not value compared to net worth. Just value, period.

ON MOTIVATING STAFF MEMBERS: It is said there are two ways to motivate people—rewards and punishments. Of the two, I would much rather have the ability to reward people than to punish them. When I was at GSA, in Washington, the inability to fire or punish people was not nearly so frustrating to me as the inability to reward those who deserved it. In private business, I had the power to give bonuses for exceptional performance, and that produced excellent work. Some of my store managers made as much every year from bonuses as they did from their base salaries. We tried to do that in Washington, but it didn't work well, because we were limited to $1,000 per year, per employee, in bonuses.

One thing that did work was saying "hello" to our 35,000 GSA employees. I wanted to send each one a birthday card, as I had done in the Eckerd Corporation, but our attorneys said that violated some federal law, even if I paid for them.

I enjoyed making unannounced visits into remote parts of our nationwide complex. I learned a lot from these visits, and it was surprising how often an employee would tell me, "Gosh, I've worked for the GSA for twenty years, and this is the first time I ever met my boss!"

If I can reward an individual for good work, I don't need to worry about punishing people for bad work. That usually takes care of itself.

ON GIVING UP CIGARETTES: I quit smoking about eight times, long before we knew that it causes cancer. It was one of the hardest things I ever did. I finally quit for good with Ruth when she was pregnant and I heard from a doctor at a party that her smoking would be bad for the baby. Here's how it happened:

I was riding in a car with Harry Roberts, my company president, one day, about twenty years ago, when both of us were trying to stop smoking. I bummed a cigarette off him, smoked half of it, and threw it out the window. I challenged him: "I'll bet you a thousand bucks you'll smoke another cigarette before I will." (That was back when a thousand bucks was a lot of money.) He was the kind of fellow who would actually pay up on a bet like that, and so was I. The next morning, he told me the bet was on, and since that day I have never smoked another cigarette, and—I know Harry well enough to know—he hasn't either. That bet did the trick, because I don't care how much I am ever worth, that first cigarette is never going to be worth a thousand bucks, so I will never smoke it.

ON CONTRACTS WITH TOP STAFF: I have never had contracts with people who worked for me. I don't think I would ever want a contract if I were working for anyone else, either. If a working relationship doesn't satisfy both parties, you're better off just breaking it up and moving on. If it is satisfactory, nobody needs a contract anyway. If you work for me and you want to leave, you should be free to leave. If I don't need you, you shouldn't want to be here.

ON ADVISING A NOVICE POLITICIAN: If some bright young person came to me today and said, "I want to run for governor," the first question I would ask would be, "Where are you going to get the financial backing?"

That may be the least understood element, by the general public, of what it takes to run and win today. I don't care how good you are, you're not going to get elected unless you have the money to compete on a somewhat even basis. And if you are running against an incumbent, he has many places to tap that you won't have. Before a new candidate gets too excited about the platform and all that, he's got to have a lot of people writing checks.

ON HIS HANDS-ON MANAGEMENT STYLE: I always loved being close to the nuts-and-bolts operation of my company, and I've noticed lots of top leaders share that. Twenty years ago I talked with Kemmit Wilson, the CEO of Holiday Inns, about a partnershp. He was one of the most amazing guys you'll ever meet. He took me to his headquarters, where they had just installed their new computerized reservations system. He acted like a kid with a toy. It was late at night, and he went into the computer room, kidding around with the computer operators. He sat down at a machine and said, "Let's see, Jack, you're down there in Clearwater. Let's say you want six rooms for tomorrow night; let's see if we can get it for you down in Clearwater." He punched it into the machine, getting some help from the staff; he loved it.

He took me down to the basement where Holiday Inns had its

printing plant. He walked around there, at almost midnight, calling the machine operators by their first names, taking a look at their work. It was wonderful.

Show me a company whose CEO spends a lot of time in the field, talking to nonmanagement people, and I'll show you a probable winner.

The biggest frustration I had with getting big was that I lost that personal contact. In the early days, I knew the store managers, their wives and kids, where they came from. That made the drugstore business enjoyable. Then it got to where I knew only the managers and supervisors, and eventually didn't even know all of them. It took a lot of the satisfaction out of it.

ON MIXING BUSINESS WITH POLITICS: Before I got into politics the first time, I had always heard that if I ran for office, it would hurt business in our drugstores. The fear was that those people who disagreed with Jack Eckerd's politics would register their disapproval by not shopping in Eckerd drugstores.

It didn't work out that way. If anything, our drugstore business got better when I was in the campaign. In all my years in politics, I never received a letter from anyone saying, "I heard your statement on television, and I don't like what you said, so I'm not going to your drugstore again." Never. People may not have agreed with my politics—obviously many of them didn't—but it didn't affect where they shopped.

My friends also warned me that if I got into politics, my good reputation would be dragged through the mud. "They'll tar and feather you, Jack, they'll crucify you." Their fears were unfounded. In three statewide campaigns, I was never crucified. They took a few shots at me, but I never got smeared.

If more businessmen understood that, they might be less reluctant to enter politics, and that would be good for the whole system. The same is true with administrative jobs in government—businessmen need to be reassured that they can give a few years to this type of public service without damaging their businesses or their reputations.

ON MINORITY MANAGERS: In the South, even many years ago when some might have guessed otherwise, black store managers were well accepted by the public in our stores. Some of our front-office staff were a little nervous when we appointed our first black managers, thinking they might not be accepted. That turned out to be baloney.

When I first moved down from Delaware and we put in our first soda fountain, the manager came to me and asked if we were going to serve blacks.

I just laughed: "Of course we are."

He protested mildly, "Lots of people think it'll hurt our business."

I said, "Well, lots of people are wrong lots of times." And that was the end of it. Serving blacks didn't hurt us at all; that's not just my opinion—that soda fountain made money from the day we opened.

ON CHRISTIANS IN POLITICS: When a Christian goes to the polls to vote, I think the faith—or lack of faith—of the candidates should be a factor, but certainly not the only factor. To insist that a Christian should vote for another Christian to the exclusion of other qualities is foolish, in my opinion. If the only thing in a person's platform is that he is a Christian, that makes me suspicious to start with. All other things being equal, I would vote for my Christian brother, of course, if he really is a Christian with a serious personal commitment to the Lordship of Jesus Christ. A candidate might call himself a Christian, but be the way I was for so many years, a "second generation" Christian, whose faith is more in a church than in what Christ did for us at the cross.

ON COMPETITION: I love to compete; I always have. I think that was probably the most enjoyable part of business to me, beating my competitors. I have been quoted as saying that when I was active in business, I hated my competitors. Well, I think I was misquoted on that. I didn't mean that I hated them personally, but I did hate the idea of losing to them, and that comes pretty close sometimes.

I also will admit that I never allowed myself to forget that tough competition had brought our country a level of quality and service unknown to the rest of the world. So I didn't want to get so cozy with other people in the drugstore business that I forgot that the whole goal of our company was to beat them. That's a large part of what business is all about, as far as I'm concerned.

I'm as competitive as ever; there has simply been a shift in my focus. Now I don't take so much personal delight in beating a competitor in the business world. Competition to me now is trying to do things better than others are doing them, and that element is still there in my life. It's just that now I find it in running a foundation or prison industries or playing tennis.

ON BEING A WORKAHOLIC: I don't think I am a workaholic. I have been called that a lot, I am aware, but to me a workaholic is someone who is driven, possessed by his work. Ruth was too smart to ever let me get into that trap.

I have always done what I enjoyed. Isn't that what you're supposed to do when you retire? So now that I'm "retired" if what I enjoy is working, it seems that I ought to be able to keep doing that, too. If a fellow gets his kicks playing golf or fishing, then that's how he ought to spend his time. It just happens that I have always gotten my kicks walking into drugstores or making an agency run or going to the camps for youngsters, which we support. Does that make me a workaholic? I don't think so.

ON EXECUTIVE PERKS: I never have done a very good job at squeezing the tax code for all the loopholes because I never have worked hard at it.

One reason is that once we went public, I decided I would never do anything that was not completely fair to the stockholders. I don't condemn someone who charges to his business his social club or golf-course membership, for example, but I just never felt they were cost effective in running drugstores.

The second reason is that I really believe it pays to lead by example, and information on that sort of thing gets around in a company. It was just a lot easier for me, when a new vice-president asked, "What are the perks?" for me to say, "Look, you won't have any, and if it's any consolation, I don't, either."

ON CHILDREN IN THE FAMILY BUSINESS: I had no particular desire for them to be part of my company, because I thought being the boss's child would be a heavy load for them to carry. None of them ever asked. Maybe they thought it would be a hard act to follow, or perhaps they wanted to show me they could do it on their own. They've done pretty well.

If I had children who entered the company, I would have tried hard to treat them based purely on their job performance, and I realize that would have been very hard to do. I'm not so sure I could have done it. And if my child had worked for the company and failed, maybe through no fault of his own, maybe he just wouldn't have the goods—well, it would be agony to sit down and tell him that. It's bad enough to do it with someone who is not a relative. I did it many times, and it was tough. It's tough to sit down with someone who has really tried, and say, "I'm sorry, but the job has to be done, so we're going to find someone else."

I'm not sure I could have done that with a son, but I would have tried, because to be fair to the stockholders and to the other people on the management team, that's the way it's gotta be.

ON CHECKS AND BALANCES IN A PUBLIC COMPANY: By the end of 1983, the Jack Eckerd Corporation was heading for trouble. Instead of being number one in our industry, we were number five and in the total chain retail field were number sixteen. By 1983 our drugstore growth had slowed to a walk. Our junior department stores and Home Video stores were going nowhere.

In 1985, disaster really struck with a bad sales year compounded by poor inventory control. By now the stock-market analysts were rightly asking whether Eckerd management and board of directors knew what we were doing.

The stock price sank, then corporate raiders moved in, and in order to protect the interest of shareholders, associates, and customers, the board was forced to seek a "white knight" who could buy us out in a friendly takeover. This effort failed, and the best remaining alternative was to sell the company to an investor group that included members of management and that would allow all employees to become indirect shareholders through the company profit-sharing plan. This transaction was completed in April, 1986.

This was a bitter pill to swallow for some of us 35,000 stockholders, who overwhelmingly approved the sale. For the first time in almost fifty years, I owned no part of an Eckerd drugstore. The fact that unsatisfactory performance by management and the board of directors (on which I played a prominent role) was responsible didn't make it any easier.

I have finally come to the conclusion that in the case of most large public companies, except for the CEO, management should not be on the board. This is rarely the case today, but in business, most companies who achieve outstanding success have to dare to be different.

Since the board of directors is really there to represent the interests of the stockholders, should the CEO be chairman of the board? As a professional manager, doesn't he have a conflict of interest? How can he represent shareholders and impartially sit in judgment on himself? I wore both hats in my time, and my successor, Stew Turley, has also done so, and I am sure we both at all times had the best interests of our stockholders in mind, but conflicts of interest are bound to arise.

The bottom line is that there were few checks or balances exercised on the power of the CEO in our company, and I don't think we were any different from most others.

ON SAILING: The sport that "hooked" me more than any other was ocean racing. It is difficult to explain the attraction of this particular sport. Someone once was asked to explain how North Atlantic Ocean racing felt, and replied: "Imagine standing under a cold shower, fully clothed, tearing up thousand dollar bills!"

My boat was the *Panacea*; she was built for cruising, not racing, but we discovered she was exceptionally fast, so we got into racing. My captain was Harold Balcom, who was just about the only guy I can recall who lived most of his life at sea and never drank, cussed, told dirty jokes, or ran around. His major weakness was that he was a lousy cook. Everyone in the sailing fraternity loved and respected Harold; he was a good man to have aboard when the weather turned foul. I was the navigator; we won a lot of races, and competed for ten years in the SORC (Southern Ocean Racing Competition) circuit.

ON CHRISTIANS IN BUSINESS: I recently bought stock in Servicemaster, a company that provides services to hospitals, colleges, plants, and homes. They have had good growth, but my decision to invest in them was based more on their "objectives," which are boldly proclaimed on page two of their annual report. Here they are:

1. to honor God in all we do
2. to help people develop
3. to pursue excellence
4. to grow profitably

Most good business managers follow the last three—but that first one is radical. Following number one is a big help when you have to make the really tough decisions.

ON FREE ADVICE: It has been truly said that free advice is usually worth what you paid for it. The readers of this book need to keep that in mind before accepting any advice found within its pages!

However, there is one exception to that—one subject on which I can give advice with total confidence, and that is on the positive results of accepting Jesus Christ as Lord of one's life. As a veteran retailer, that is one prescription on which I will gladly give a money-back guarantee.

Afterword

Chuck Colson

Jack Eckerd is typical of that special breed of Americans whose exploits in the business world are legendary. He was a hard-driving, hardheaded, highly competitive entrepreneur who made it to the top. He was never content unless he was winning, always prodded by the thrill of the chase, the love of the competition. He took risks in business, just as he did in flying, and he always beat the odds and came out a winner.

But it was not enough. It never is. Something was missing. Deep inside Jack Eckerd, as in every man and woman, there was a vacuum success could not fill; it was an emptiness that was satisfied only by the presence of God, as eventually Eckerd came to realize.

The need for God is universal; it is a fundamental fact that all of us, sooner or later, must confront. With some individuals, that need is obscured by the illusion that, if only we acquire enough money, enough power, enough fame—then we will find the inner satisfaction we crave.

If success will satisfy, Jack Eckerd should have been a totally satisfied man. He had it all—money, family, reputation, success, health, power, you name it—and it was not enough. His very achievements exposed success as the false god that it is.

What makes Eckerd's testimony even more significant is that he was never a "bad" man in the conventional sense. His story is not that of the derelict who met God after bouncing off the bottcm of a misspent life. To the contrary, Eckerd was a very "good" man long before he began to take God seriously—honest, loyal, good husband and father, generous, concerned citizen, church member.

But Eckerd came to realize that being a "good" man in that sense was not the point. For one thing, our "goodness" is nothing in God's eyes—and no matter how "good" we are on the outside, every human on the inside is filled with envy, hatred, ill-feelings— yes, *sin* that we can do nothing about.

Eckerd realized as well that he had never faced the greatest question in life: "Who is Jesus Christ, and what am I going to do about Him?" In almost seventy years he had never been forced to face that question. When he finally did so, it changed his life; by his own testimony, it brought a richness and a meaning to his life that makes all his earlier accomplishments and pleasures pale in comparison.

When he gave Christ control of his life, Jack Eckerd changed. Friends who have known him for many years describe him as more at peace with himself, less impatient with others, better able to love and be loved. His employees can see it; his secretary of many years has remarked that he is a totally different person. Even his family has found the new Jack Eckerd very different from the old one.

Eckerd himself describes the change as an internal one; he does some of the same things as before, he says, but his motives are different. His ego is coming under control, he says, and he is learning how to do whatever he does for the glory of Christ rather than the glory of Jack Eckerd. I've seen this firsthand over and over in his life.

One such example is what happened a few days after his conversion, when Eckerd walked into one of his drugstores. He looked at the magazine racks, which he had seen thousands of times before, but this day he saw them through new eyes. He was horrified to find *Playboy* and *Penthouse* on sale in his "family" stores.

Jack returned to his office and called the company CEO. "How about taking these magazines out?" The executive offered to investigate, even though the magazines brought in several million dollars a year. Eckerd insisted, and management concurred. So within days, *Playboy* and *Penthouse* were removed from the bookracks of 1,700 Eckerd drugstores across America.

I called Jack and asked if he had done this because of conversion to Christ. "Of course," he replied. "Why else would I throw a few million dollars out the window?" Then he continued, "The reason was simple: the Lord wouldn't let me off the hook."

What a magnificent answer; the most learned theologian couldn't give a more eloquent description of the Lordship of Christ.

But that wasn't the end. Jack wrote to the presidents of other drug chains, describing what he had done, testifying that it hadn't killed him, and nudging then in the same direction. No one answered his letters; after all, pornography is a profitable business.

But encouraged by Eckerd's asking, thousands of Christians, organized under the National Coalition Against Pornography, were taking their stand as well—through widespread picketing and a boycott of stores selling "adult magazines."

The pressure began to pay off. Like dominoes, stores began to remove *Playboy* and *Penthouse*: one by one, Revco, People's, Rite Aid, Dart Drug, Gray Drug and High's Dairy Stores all pulled pornography from their shelves.

Finally, the last major holdout gave in as well: 7–11 removed pornography from its 4,500 stores and recommended that its 3,600 franchises do the same.

For two decades, citizen groups have worked to stop the spread of pornography. Presidential commissions have recommended legislation, but Congress had been slow to act. The ACLU has successfully challenged in the courts most of the laws that have been passed. Nothing has worked. As an ACLU spokesman boasted after the last presidential commission report, "there are enough constitutional questions here to litigate for the next twenty years."

What couldn't be accomplished by passing laws or fighting in courts was accomplished when a man gave his life to Christ and surrendered to His Lordship. The pornography industry is on the run; in the last year smut has been eliminated from 15,000 retail outlets—and it all started with Jack Eckerd's conversion. Don't tell me one man can't make a difference!

This is the way God has always worked—not through institutions and governments, but through individuals He has chosen.

I believe Jack Eckerd's conversion is one of the most significant of our generation. Not only is he one of the most respected businessmen in America, but he is not accustomed to being silent and passive on those matters about which he feels deeply.

His influence is being felt not just in the pornography battle but in the field of criminal justice reform as well. As a member of the board of directors, Jack has given invaluable leadership to my ministry—and to other prison ministries as well. He is in the vanguard of reform efforts like PRIDE—the model prison industries program he leads in his own state—and in revamping state criminal justice systems as he did so successfully in Florida in 1983.

Jack Eckerd is living proof that one man can make a difference. Jesus Christ made a difference in him, and now with God's help, he is making a difference in his world. That is what the gospel is all about, for Jack Eckerd and for every one of us.